Love
Labor
Liberation

Love
Labor
Liberation
IN LASANA SEKOU

Howard A. Fergus

House of Nehesi Publishers
P.O. Box 460
Philipsburg, St. Martin
Caribbean

WWW.HOUSEOFNEHESIPUBLISH.COM

ISBN: 978-0-913441-87-9
LC Control Number: 2007936719

Author's acknowledgments: Thanks are due to Fiona Meade, Teresina Fergus, and Nylvae Woodley for typing the manuscript and to the University of the West Indies Centre in Montserrat for its general and generous assistance.

Cover, graphics design by Gina Rombley
Cover art: *Bounty*, by Drisana Deborah Jack, © Deborah Jack.
Photography: Saltwater Collection, Drisana Deborah Jack

Love and labor conquer all things.

- Joseph H. Lake, Sr.

Contents

Preface

Born in Aruba in 1959, and reared in St. Martin from infancy to age 13, Harold Hermano Lake adopted the name by which he is now universally known: Lasana Mwanza Sekou. This name and name change, while he was a high school student in New York, is consonant with his acute sense of his African roots, his worldview, and a lifelong mission as a liberator using the weapons of creative writing talents and impressive scholarship. After studying and sojourning in the United States of America from 1972 to 1984, he claimed St. Martin of kinship connections as his home. Owned by two European countries, St. Martin was a fit base from which to send forth revolutionary waves with a global reach. Author of some 12 books of poetry and other imaginative writings, Sekou is one of the most prolific Caribbean poets. Some may detect the influence of other writers on Sekou, but the voice that reaches us is *sui generis*, unique and Sekouesque. Themes recur, but there is no staleness and never want for excitement.

To refer to Sekou as a miracle of St. Martin is not to cleverly contrive a literary device, which he often uses to functional effect; it is not to underrate St. Martin with the wonder that something good can come out of it; it is not to say big cannot come from small since Aimé Césaire and Frantz Fanon are testaments against this. It is to grope for a handle to capture the stature and status of this literary icon from, yes, a small divided island; it is to recognize that Sekou's vision of liberation was born in St.

Martin, and even though Aruba gave him birth, and his playground is the world, home is here, as Jamaica's Dennis Scott says:

> Here to the sand where sleep belongs
> I come as quietly as children
> into the harbour of your love . . .
> the salt that frosts so many other faces[1]

Only, Sekou does not come quietly, and as a writer he has matured beyond his years. This is an aspect of the miracle. He was turning water and St. Martin's salt into the wine of literary astonishment at a tender age. In his mouth, both scribal and oral, the word was becoming flesh and the flesh word. The breadth and depth of his output, his encyclopedic knowledge, his dream to change the world beginning with St. Martin, and his comfort with a range of genres are together too marvelous for words—especially ours, ordinary mortals'. There is some justification, therefore, for calling Sekou a miracle. So Oyoko Loving, the St. Croix poet rightly asserts, "St. Maarten has produced a miracle."[2] Love, labor, and liberation are identified as major themes, but these subsume others such as family life, education, patriotism, national and international heroes, culture, and more. In fact, culture as the basis and guiding star of development is Sekou's preoccupation and cries out for some focus. A major purpose of his work is to build a counterculture or, better yet, a new culture as the foundation of independence without discarding tested values and upful folk knowledge.

Do not expect love, labor, and liberation to be discrete

entities; they are more like a continuum serving the writer's purpose, interconnecting. Who can keep a river from flooding sometimes and in some seasons overflowing its banks? Sekou's writings are like a rapturous and restless, river, sometimes muddy, sometimes placid, always deep. He will not abide strict categories—not even *performance poet*—if this will obscure the intellectualism, the functional visual techniques, literary depth, and serious purpose.

This brief opening piece is correctly called a *preface*, for the entire volume is an introduction to Sekou's work as poet, storyteller, presenter of dramatic monologues, and essayist. Hopefully, it is somewhat worthy of this great person, his purpose, and his philosophy. He articulates his vision and artistic yea, his life's purpose clearly in several of his pieces. Here is one such passage from "For Summer Only" in his third poetry collection *Images in the Yard* (1983), also cited by Musa W. Ibrahim in his introduction to it:

Children
The Sun is upon us
Come
Let us go
Out into the yard and play
Into the streets
And love
Into the fields
And labor
Coming into our own
Fighting for rights
By all means necessary

In "to task" in *Mothernation - Poems from 1984 to 1987* (1991), he again adumbrates the task: "Like I told my love the other day / there are much hands to set about work" and "There are power sounds / like gwoka, still to set free."

The burden of the poems is also the burden of the prose. A character in *Brotherhood of the Spurs* (1997) tells us unequivocally, "Man must know he is here to labor and lowe [*love*], to battle for right and build that which is right." So the themes recur and intermingle; significantly, he ends the preface of that unique national primer on St. Martin, that must-read national text, *National Symbols of St. Martin: A Primer* (1996), like an exhorter ending his discourse with the literal bottom line, the underpinning message: Love, Labor, Liberation. In studying these themes and something of their richness, we are exploring the man, the mission, and the message and why he speaks so effectively. In so doing, we are exploring the cultural geography of St. Martin, and for Sekou, there are parallel St. Martins across the Caribbean and the world. They are his burden too. I hope you find the journey as exciting, enlightening, and emotionally charged as I have found it. I purport to bring to the task a reverence worthy of this human and humanitarian wonder, this "rapidly rising star in the firmament of Caribbean writers."[3]

Howard A. Fergus
Montserrat

1

LOVE

"Conventional" Relationships

Lasana M. Sekou was never sick of love in Solomonic terms, but he was and is preoccupied with its mysteries and meanings, and he found it a powerful metaphor for life, creativity, and development. Love, for him, is about birth and destiny, among other things. It is significant that his first volume (published in his late teens) contains a section on love, and so does the second. Love is not just synonymous with lust; it is not just romantic liaison, not just a collision of bodies, intentional or by chance. Linda Taylor's judicious warning nearly 30 years ago is even more applicable today. Relative to love in *Moods for Isis - Picture poems of Love & Struggles* (1978) she wrote, "I warn you to enter with caution; for . . . the spirit of love mingles freely with the spirit of Revolution and progress."[1] At the outset of this chapter on love *á la* Sekou, we do well to mark this. Contrary to the subhead, there is very little that is conventional about Sekou's treatment of love.

We cannot say that Sekou is a poet of love, full stop, in the same manner as we can say William Wordsworth is a poet of nature. For in Sekou, love may not be always many-splendored, but it is many-sided, and the sides interconnect. He understands heterosexual love in its naked beauty even though the lair is sometimes obscured by coverlets of lush language; he understands pure love that creates families and nations; he understands the naughtiness of love that fails and redemptive love on earth as it is in heaven; and he understands brotherly love. Love is indeed a unifying and pervading theme, which becomes the matrix of much of his work.

If the photographs of divas who decorate the pages of *Moods for Isis* are any indication, Sekou has an eye and a heart for beauty, and many desirable Eves (one suspects that he archly plays on the word "eve" in "Virgo Girl") people his paradise. "Summer Love" is about two lovers obviously coupling beginning with the foreplay of exploration with "honey-dipped" kisses leading to orgasmic ecstasy with legs rubbing and other pleasurable action in between *en route* to "lovedom." There is shared climactic joy, too, in "Today."

How bountiful Love was today!!
. . .
Now all is well
The gentle throbbing
Has washed yesterday's pain away

The ending jolts to reality and dulls sentimentality.

This device is deliberately used by the poet to curb mawkishness. In "city of poetry" of *37 Poems* (2005), there are no brakes on the luxuriating language and brimming emotion:

> she wanders to the dryness of his unsuspecting body,
> pressing herself hungrily
> until he and she and sheet reach in the deep soak,
> a wanton geography sea

But the loving here is more about the muse of poetic creation than about physical copulation. The graphic visual and visceral imagery he employs in some poems illustrates both his range of creative tools and his range of perceptions of love. He writes about the cock breaking the "hymen of spread-legged dawn / inviting us to lick open destiny's lips to orgasmic sight" in "The cubs are in the field" (1999) with the same ease as about a couple reaching deep soak and with a different effect. Love is a fertile mine of imageries. Even here love is almost sacramental, purifying, leading to wholeness, and the raw pleasure of love is attenuated by language; in "Summer Love" the summit of the love experience is like a "nectar from heaven." And we should not heedlessly bypass the tough graphic statement which ends the poem: "As she sank downstairs / To pretend / . . . . nothing was happening." This treatment of lovemaking is not surprising, for it is never to be indiscriminate. In this young volume, he is interested in the difference between love and lust as "Beware Lover" indicates. There is a difference between love and the mere feeling of infatuation: "Did love answer / or did lust question?" is a question put to a young lover. Sekou is amazingly consistent with his themes and philosophies. Nineteen years after *Moods for Isis* in "The Wake," a short story from *Brotherhood of the Spurs*, Cyus, a community elder who is also the ahead-of-his years Sekou, is at pains to make the distinction between enduring love and fleeting fancies.

As the poet matured, his treatment of the romantic experience is even more subtle. He goes beyond the erotic rubbing of legs or "Ayana" following "my moves with thirstful chants" and in "Sunspice" where "I, Mighty Cobra / Swell between your tender thighs" in *For the Mighty Gods . . . An Offering* (1982). In *The Salt Reaper – Poems from the flats* (2004), "home again" is one such poem: subtle, polished, artistically complete, where, in spite of "dancing between the legs of a demon,"

there is no embrace.no touch to say
the what she does to me. her eyes. her smile. /
her yes. yearn.

And yet there is no doubt about consummation conveyed by telling symbols "from the hilly bushes and up / from the chilly sea / from all around the salted pond." This is pure magic. As Hollis "Chalk-dust" Liverpool observes in an erudite introduction, this comes from a book that begins with "No Love Poems" and the line "There will be no love poems to-night." It suits Sekou's purpose well. No love poems mean rejecting a soft position, opiate religiosity, and a snow-white culture. He is not rejecting his kind of poetry but the conventional kind. In fact, in his hand, the poem becomes a vehicle of a serious agenda, of assault and of protest:

> There will be no love poems tonight
>> only sweaty words
>> pond salt rhymes
>> calloused complaints from people's voices

Another love poem of the mature years worth cit-ing is "last night" from *37 Poems*. It is striking for its unobtrusive rhymes, its economy of language, in-cluding the felicitous and powerfully simple last line. The poem's last two lines, "i look / no more" convey the harrowing silence of disappointment and finality. Here, unrequited love is deftly delivered with genu-ine emotion.

It is only a short step from making a distinction between love and lust to singing the praises of pure love, and Sekou the idealist makes that step. This is remarkable at his age. In "And" from his book of "genesis," he reflects:

and if our love be pure
then on meeting
after a day's absence
feel how stronger
our embrace will be
twice as passionate
our hearts . . . . . .

The purity of love is a measure of its quality and endurance. "In Another Song For You" from *Images in the Yard* (1983), he laments the disgusting spectacle of love and lust going hand-in-hand and their perpetrators missing the truth that with the purity of love . . . "we shall live forever." Pure love is of course the partner of devotion and commitment, and the summit of mutuality.

This love thing
An isle of demandless devotion
Carrying us away
Without care

That is how it is presented in "This Love Thing" from *Images in the Yard*; "A Last Love Song" in *Born Here* (1986) is a threnody of commitment to the loved one with that quality of love that washes away incompleteness. "Love Poem," also in *Born Here*, smacks of a kind of purity, too, where although it is a long time coming, the passion seems to burn up in singing of loving rather than in ravishing the loved one. In "No-

Cat" from the same volume, love is a joyous occasion linked with laughter, but its purpose is the sharing of this life's burden. In these poems the preoccupation is with love as an idea rather than a run for the sheets.

It bears repetition that love for Sekou transcends a physical engagement. The "pure" love poems as "Africanita Dushi" in *Born Here* are a rarity where for the man "There is no where to go now / But inside," and the woman will have no greater pleasure,

Than to feast
To come again
To rise with me
To the crown of Paradise Hill

Yet, this supposedly pure love poem ends with the lines: "Woman / This is you and I" which speak of coupling unity that strikes one as more than physical. That is the point. Love in Sekou is metaphysical, indeed spiritual; and I discern in his love poems a marked resemblance to the work of the English metaphysical poets of the seventeenth century such as George Herbert and John Donne. Their love poems are characterized by a pleasing, even if at times jolting, blend of feeling and ratiocination or a tough intellectualism if you prefer. The reader must not be surprised to see comparisons made between Sekou's work and the writings of illustrious poets, for there is nothing simple or simplistic about his work. I would not be surprised if the greatest recognition comes after his demise, as happens all too often. It is comforting to say a man is ahead of his times, but it is up to critics and reviewers to draw quality attention to Sekou's work. This is crucial, especially for him whose work has a revolutionary and educative purpose and is informed by cogent issues of contemporary society and history.

After that irresistible diversion, let me illustrate the metaphysical nature of some of the poems. "Growing" in *Moods for Isis* is logically about love as growth, but it is the merging of two persons through physical contact into one that is metaphysical: "Yes .... I could love / Until both our beings / Merge into oneness." This ultimate union of spirits, a subset of beings, is as mystical as marriage. To clinch the point, we have these lines from the same book:

How then can I tell you .... of whom I love
Of the she that I have shared my body with
And have given
Of my mind and manhood[2]

Shakespeare, too, wrote of the marriage of two minds in one of his sonnets. The oneness of lovers recurs in "And" in *Moods for Isis*: "our bodies / coming together / ... / feel the absence of matter / and so .... melt into each other." This phenomenon is also evident in *Images in the Yard*. In "Twilight of This Love," the soul does the longing for "One Love / One heart." The poem "Love Dancing" in the same volume takes this further and deeper. Love is almost sacramental. Real love is holy, eroticism and all; "Who knows what songs to sing / When approaching the burning bush" is so powerfully suggestive of the divine and of a holy environment. The lesson supposedly is that it is humans who have tainted sex. Written a little later, *Born Here* takes love directly to a sacred Christian ceremony. The man must not leave the lover "Without the memory / Of a last supper." The lines resonate with the sacramental and even the sacrificial. Never mind that there is an irrepressible suggestion here that love involves loss and death. Sekou leaves us in no doubt that love is a most complex emotion.

One trait of the metaphysical poet's love pieces was the tough surprising imagery and its intellectual demand: "could there be a prayer / so like the captive fleece of silver in your hair" scarcely sounds like a love poem, but it is, or for that matter:

and revel over your corpulence fine and pout
though not to consume you just yet
but to worship in vulgar disregard
at the mounds to paradise descent,

where words and phrases such as "captive fleece," "paradise descent," and "pout" can be invested with so much thoughtful meaning and where the juxtaposition of "worship" and "vulgar" heightens the emotions. The quotations are from a poem entitled "intoxicate" from *The Salt Reaper*. In *37 Poems* "mariposa" also has easy liquid movement where "love is fine and full / ... / and everybody else but you / makes bad coffee" with its novel imaging and surprise ending could easily have been written by a metaphysical poet. From, my perspective then, Sekou's love poetry is metaphysical in a double sense. Perhaps it is metaphysical, too, in a deeper spiritual sense in that the result of physical union is the foetus of new horizons. The lyrically beautiful "Love Majesty" in *Born Here* illustrates this and is truly worth a quote in its own right as an elegant love piece.

> Come morning
> I will walk with you
> On the rim of dawn
> Lay before the first light
> And together
> Born a new day ...

It is worth remarking on Sekou's revulsion against warped love and the incidence of the deprivation of love. Love is never to be trivialized in his view, so from the onset, in *Moods for Isis*, he is against children having children for the fun of it; or in his words, "In an act of play." There is also zero tolerance for those who think "Loving / Was what you do / When there is nothing else."[3] He laments the nonlove that unites persons only in vices like booze, cigarettes, and a protruding beer belly. The word "love" appears only in the title of "They Claim to Love Each Other" in *Moods for Isis*, but its absence in the poem deafeningly proclaims the absence of love in certain relationships. In the very next poem "Orphan," the problem of children deprived of love is highlighted, and this has implications for family life and productivity.

Beyond the unity of love between couples, Sekou is keen on corporate love: the love of the brotherhood. One can hardly do better at the outset than to agree with Dr. Joanna Rummens' insightful comment on the story "Brotherhood of the Spurs," which gives the book its title: "This story thus represents a culmination of Sekou's love theme, an appeal to the notion of brotherhood which, one might argue, constitutes the highest and truest form of love."[4]

Dr. Rummens' assertion that brotherhood is the true form of love may be arguable; that it represents a culmination of the love theme is most tenable. Sekou was young in years when he published *Moods for Isis*, but there is nothing so green about it. A seminal work, it is like a fertile ground with multiple seeds that sprout and blossom later. Like Rummens, Taylor remarked on the poet's interest in brotherhood.[5] She cites "Sir Harry J" in which the veteran of that name conspires with and expresses solidarity with young poets. (The poet grabs the opportunity to honor the noble bearing and sagacity of this black warrior-statesman.) "Love One Another" in *Images in the Yard* is a warm and patent exhortation on brotherhood: "togetherness" and the sharing of trials and triumphs. As spiritual brothers, they

Carry our burdens
Our crosses
Our corpses
Our fears and our tears

The tone of the poet is somber, betraying perhaps his consciousness of sacrifice in revolutionary brotherhood and the regrettable necessity of trashing "The chaff from the grain."

Where brotherhoods bound by love do not exist, they must be created and without tolerance of any generation gap. "Solidarity" in *Mothernation - Poems from 1984 to 1987* (1991) calls for a gathering "in critical mass numbers, marchers / great and small" and to form human "ring ropes" around "our earth" and around St. Martin's treasure, including its people. And brotherhood is transnational as "Visit&Fellowship I" in *The Salt Reaper* suggests. There is a love that binds fellow revolutionaries; and when "I am here / in Miami" one is closer to Fidel and Aristide and, by extension, many others in the

Caribbean, the Americas, and Africa. Finally, culture is brotherhood linking "us with we is we all / over / shares us, Romare Bearden collaging us" and the us includes one of his icons, poet and historian, Kamau Brathwaite.[6]

The Ideal Loved One

Sekou's ideal love is rooted and patriotic. Given his general philosophy of black self-affirmation and what some refer to as negritude, it should be no surprise that Africa features strongly in Sekou's concept of love and beauty. Thus, in *Born Here* "Makeda" may be Papiamentu- or Spanish-speaking, but she is an African queen, gentle, with songs in her eyes. And "Woman" on the next page associated with Dominica is ascribed the bearing of a goddess. Words like "pearl" and "goddess" and the general poetic descriptions, bespeak an ideal beauty even if they have the effect of distancing the love experience from real flesh and blood. In "Woman" the lady's dark lips (and note her lips are necessarily dark) are "Softer than the breath of falling dew." And although "Africanita" in *For the Mighty Gods*, is bathed with passion, as the wind sings the praises of the beloved and carry her scent, it can easily be a personification of Africa.

Sekou is no indiscriminate racist even though he obviously loves his race, else he would not be Sekou.

He is large-hearted enough to recognize, indeed to celebrate, human worth and value and beauty in any nation. The critic Tabish Khair recognizes this in his introduction to *37 Poems* when he insists that "xinX-in," penned in China, is essentially a love poem. In that poem, Sekou's "Love is also combined with larger concerns" and its "narration of seeing and not-seeing retains a subterranean seam of significance that would repay critical digging."[7] From his early poems, the beautiful female is bedecked with the usual "pearls" of words. She is, in his own words, "moon-face majesty," she has celestial curves and his description of her thighs as "twin pillars" resonates Solomon's *Song of Songs*. Yet even if there is a suggestion that she is lily white or "she like chocolatina," she is the essence of African beauty and her voluptuous body tells of black glory. Thus, in *The Salt Reaper* we find "about a drink," where "the bogota blond / shaped like a nok figurine" and "the tobago black soft to serene" are exuding in essence Sekou's African beauty ideal. An early poem cast in a similar mold in *For the Mighty Gods* is "Lady D.M.," a stage setter. One is not sure whether the poem sings a song of love or of the loved one because she is sometimes ethereal and paradisiacal; in the end she resembles "an Afrikan Goddess of love." What is beyond doubt is that African women such as Sheba and Iyangura are for him pearls of great beauty. In

"For Debbie" from *Images in the Yard* we get a sense of Sekou's ideal womanhood. Not only is she African, but she is stamped with African imagery. She is a Nile flower, and she moves to the rhythm of Congo stream and Niger river, and interestingly, not much, if anything, is lost in her westward trek to Belize—a hint of the author's Pan-Africanism. In fact, Africa is home, and these western lands constitute an African diaspora; and the African woman is essential to "Giving / Birth" to liberation.[8]

That the ideal woman is black is Sekou's unabashed thesis, and the ideal woman was the original: "Truly those in the Garden / Were Africans."[9] "Beginnings," which is found in *For the Mighty Gods*, confirms that the fertile black woman was the first mother "blessed and beautiful among women"—words with the ring of a kind of virgin Mary, the mother of God. This is quite a claim but not an unusual one. No wonder then that blacks, Africans in whatever location, or certainly dark skin people, are the bearers of light in the person of a pantheon of gods: Zeus, Buddha, Krishna, and Christ. These all carry equal status, and are all carved in the likeness of the black man.

With this perspective of Africa and Africanism, Sekou is impatient with actions of self-loathing and the mimicking of "others." This lack of self-appreciation, which for Sekou betrays a deficiency in the knowledge of history, is evident in "Non-Ideological Negroes" from *Images in the Yard*. He pours scorn on liberal blacks (ironically) who mimic the enemy. And Sekou is a master of the imagery of scorn:

There you go
Stooping in shit
Crying over
A-dying-over-a-europe-dying
Lapping the scab of america's syphilis[10]

There is spitting disgust in the word choice. The gerry-curled, hair-weaved, skin-bleached woman who acerbically rejects her African or black identity and culture is exposed as being among the individuals who have lost "natural identity / of Afrika Woman," without essence and on "the road to nowhere."[11] The author feels so strongly on this issue that *Born Here* contains a poem on those "Who Hate Themselves." Embracing "Aryan arrogance," they judge themselves by an alien standard of beauty in respect to their hair, nose, and lips. Shortsighted and untutored, they cannot appreciate

Our nose
Was so lovingly spread and sculptured
In the first tender moment of creation
And our lips
For being so fully grown

and "the round ripeness of our women's behind." He dismisses these as still slaves. There is liberation in love of the Sekou kind.

The influence and language of Black American cultural nationalism and radical tradition are evident in Sekou's writings between 1978 and 1984 but the self-loathers are best contrasted with the Rastafarians or Rastafari, whom Sekou treats differently. For him, they represent African culture and pride in Africa with Ras Tafari as their messiah, Jah as the name for God and "Ithiopia" as their mecca or zion. Juxtaposed to the decadence of the gerry-curled, hair-weaved, skin-bleached posse, are the trappings of Rastafarianism: "but the locks dem lash back rude the roots dem routed from refuge to renewal&revel."[12] And consonant with Rasta and African ecology, this approved generation of black kinky hair, "I & I" can pray not only to Jesus Christ but to Ogun, Allah and Jah to at least "bless the roundest curl recurrent" in *The Salt Reaper* poem "war on the blackest hair." They are a contrast to Europhiles, men and women "Too intelligent / In their miseducation" who mimic the "pale styles" in *Images in the Yard*. Paleness here is a derogatory reference to the racist features of western cultural imperialism. The poem cited is provocatively and evocatively titled, "The Hasbeenlicktuals," one of many Sekouesque coinages, loaded with satire.

Sekou embraces Rastafarians, hopefully not un-critically, as gate keepers and exponents of African culture. They are important elements in his love affair with Africa and his Pan-Africanism. References to "de bredren" are scattered throughout his work; "See the Idren" in *Born Here* is one of his longer poems, the longest in that volume. It contains conventional Rasta thinking and paraphernalia—their reverence for a black god and their link with Garveyism, the centrality of their roots culture and the arts, "As I & I find Self in song / And all chant . . . One Love." He includes the lighting up of the communal chalice, the Bob Marley connection, and all in a reggae (Rasta) rhythm complete with a redemption song quote, "take me to the border / so I can step across." Let there be no misunderstanding, as we shall see later in this vol-ume, culture for Sekou is a strategy, and he is steeped in Rasta subculture, which he would scarcely con-sider "sub-." Rastafarians representing an alternative philosophy of life set against conventional Christian-ity symbolized by Rome, and a contaminated culture or political system symbolized by Babylon, are at the vanguard of the revolution (themes do an element of injustice to Sekou and his holistic vision of a sane society). Accordingly, they will receive Jah's inspired word: "TO CHARGE DOWN INNA BABYLON" and intriguingly to "Chant down inna Babylon." The chant is parallel to the charge and equally strong; the revolutionary weapons are both physical and mental, but I am getting ahead of myself. I must nevertheless emphasize that for Sekou, Rasta language itself suggests a revolution and a counterculture. Rasta and Sekou are truly One Love.

Love's Purpose

Sekou is not immune to the palpable pleasure of love and does not condemn worshipping at the shrine of Eros, or Oshun, under the appropriate circumstances. This is evident in his work, especially the early vintage. "Pleasure Divine" in *Moods for Isis*, also referred to by Taylor, is suffused with kissing and caressing a rich and "fertile" woman. Fertility is a critical word with Sekou because it transcends mere replenishment of the earth. True love must also result in a procreation of ideas, of the sinews of nation building, and in the blossoming of an independent nation. A supporting text can be pulled from virtually anywhere in Sekou because this is seminal (the pun is intended) to his purpose and philosophy as a revolutionary writer. "I have come . . . in request of your longing / I am here . . . there is life!"[13]

Peeking over winter's shoulder, the winter of discontent, the winter wasteland, the persona has come through love to generate life and build a common-wealth of love. Whatever else love is, it is about prog-ress and new paradigms of national development. "Love's Majesty" cited elsewhere in the chapter (and the title is instructive) has very little to do with sen-suality. Island woman goes to bed, but the purpose is to born a new day. This is reinforced in "For Glo-ria My Cousin with Love" in *Moods for Isis*, which is worth quoting at length:

> When little girls grow
> And women emerge
> The world awaits
> For them to change
> That which is old
> And give birth To a stronger love
> And better tomorrows
> To bring forth brave men
> And strong women / of beauty / -with minds
> . . .
> It should be known
> That no man is complete
> Without the woman
> No mind . . . . without the womb

What an insightful manifesto of love and birth, both of which have a political purpose; there is no doubt that the poet's intention is to produce regenerated minds.

Mind is related to consciousness, and Sekou plainly states this in the preface to *National Symbols of St. Martin – A Primer* (1996): "Indeed the labor and love ... hopes and dreams of the St. Martin people have given birth to a national consciousness." This echoes, in a way, the idea of producing minds, as is referred to in *Mothernation*[14]; and minds are closely associated with liberation that the African is compelled to birth, says a positively biased Sekou in his quest to redress past wrongs and restore order and social equilibrium.

Sekou would hardly be against selective breeding, which means sowing the right seeds. This is necessary if the revolution is to be effectively serviced. These lines from "A Kwanza Poem" in *Moods for Isis* make this abundantly clear:

> Freedom yearning eggs
> Actively waiting to be fertilized
> By black warrior sperm
> So that a revolution may be conceived.

This is such a delicious nexus of the erotic and idealistic. For every warrior and daughter of fertility, copulation must bring forth rebirth and a new day. In *Mothernation*, the hour demands

> a tropical Spring of everlasting Golden Ages
> a multiple of sun-green orgasms.[15]

In this context, a healthy family life and appropriate education are important, both of which Sekou addresses diligently in his work. In addition to the romantic element, there is no doubt what love is about in Sekou.

Love in Fiction

Sekou's stories create opportunities for elaborating and exemplifying the love theme in fictional relationships. Treating love in story and poetry demonstrates his unity of purpose and reinforces his convictions. *Love Songs Make You Cry* (1989) is by definition about love, and as Daniella Jeffry observed, love is the collection's unifying theme, appearing in sundry manifestations. One can hardly do better than reproduce here Jeffry's excellent summary of the various faces of love. The love landscape (if I may mix the metaphor) includes

> . . . The sisterhood between Elsa and Dolores, between Dolores and Maria, the "paardnership" between Roy, Freddie and Elton are of the same nature, based on reaching out to each other, helping each other in times of need. This is the real friendship of the teen years and early twenties. Flirtatious love, a kind of sensuous love, is experienced by Elsa and Wilfred, Annie and Eddie, Clement and Blair, the young man and woman of "Love Songs Make You Cry."[16]

Two of the four stories in *Brotherhood of the Spurs* allow Sekou to sustain the love theme. "The Wake" gives expression to self-sacrificing love, which entails forgiveness; commitment to family, especially children; and the redeeming power of love. In the title story, brotherhood is based on a special love that speaks to spiritual and communal bonding. As in his poetry, Agape rather than eros is exalted.

We shall now give flesh and blood to a small selection of these generalizations. In "Snoring" we have an example of perverted and adulterous love in Wilfred, who takes advantage of a swooning, immature minor in Elsa of foolish fantasies. The butt of the author's ire, the former, is in the end awarded with arrest for cocaine, "full of shit about his public image." He is a contrast to Freddie, a man after Sekou's heart, rejecting white racist perceptions of blacks; his love is homespun and genuine, and he comes to the rescue of Elsa. The statement "Freddie Jacobs was always there" says so much about constancy and reliability, and Sekou is a master of such powerful but simple-on-the-surface statements in prose as well as in verse.

"Fatty and the Big House" is melodramatic in parts, but it reveals the old-fashioned (and faithful) lover and the old-fashioned industriousness of Annie the loved one. Forgiveness is an important subtheme in Sekou, as Fatty and Annie are in the end united after she had been caught in the act. Sekou the impatient revolutionist has this softer side and can deal with a large house of human emotions and experiences, which make him credible and forgivable for occasional excesses.

There are parallels in "The Wake," where Ademus' sacrificial love for Edonia is exhibited and in this case, a mysterious revelation of truth, forgiveness comes into play, bringing about healing and "unity." Love here has a spiritual dimension and is of redemptive quality.[17] This is how Sekou would have it. He is also interested in the love of the children displayed by Ademus, even after losing his wife's affection. Still, in "The Wake" when Cyus, a Sekou proxy, tells the gathering of generations at the wake that they are one family and one people, he propagates brotherhood and brotherly love that do not brook generation gaps; this we have already identified in the poetry, as well as in the story "Brotherhood of the Spurs." In a strange way, the fighting cocks on the one hand and their sponsors on the other are brothers underlining the seeming paradox of the title. In his magnanimity, Sekou recognizes brotherhood in the two colonial territories into which his St. Martin nation is divided, between Guadeloupe and St. Martin, and by extension among the other Caribbean countries and territories at the "maroon." The fight may not be spurious, but it is artificial and ephemeral.

"Love Songs Make You Cry," the signature story of Sekou's maiden voyage into his own fictional writings, presents yet another contrast in love. The patient, dedicated love of Manny the mature man (almost to silliness) is set against the passionate love of an unnamed youth who could exemplify any woman. Kindred spirit in sensuous love, a young man was able to draw "strange cries from her body while washing her in what she knew now were the bottomless depths and lofty heights of her own desires." In this story as in the poems, Sekou is never reticent about his ideal of womanhood, which reflects respect for his forebears. Close to nature, she has "the face of a full moon (one of Sekou's favorite metaphors of bold and glowing beauty), cat-eyes set in high cheek-bones of an ancient race, Ciboney, Taino maybe; her body, of sculptured Africaninity, bearing a cool Caribbean coloring of cinnamon." Add the yellow windbreaker and yes, yes the red terry cloth headband. Details do not escape this eagle-eyed prophet.

Occasionally, passionate love in Sekou is painted with a heavy hand as he luxuriates in nature and his effusive love for words. Sekou is in love with language and music. Love on this carnival night in "Love Songs Make You Cry" is music, and the reggae-dub-rasta beat that is new to her will find itself within the young woman "like a drum symphony of sensuous waves pressing harshly, madly, firmly, gently against those secret places where the earth drinks of the sun's thirst and draws the sea into its caverns and upon its lands." This is almost like a sexual experience though the beautiful language distances it. All through Sekou's work, love transcends sex, and here he has two lovers locked in arms, exchanging fragrances, thereby dulling the carnal element and bathing both in a spiritual aura.

Amid all the sensuousness, Sekou's sense of balance and realism guarantees his credibility. He knows that love attracts irony in its bitter and sweet experiences, in its sometimes fleetingness and failure to utterly fulfill. Indeed, "Love Songs Make You Cry" with tears of joy and laughter closer than we realize, from a superficial reading. Even the dependable and durable Manny caused pain: "Manny's presence was paining her now, his silence was becoming more like a grave, dutiful and confining vigil." In "The Wake," approved elder Cyus brings another ironic twist to love. While admitting with Camille that God is love and perhaps its true source, for him love is a revengeful sword wielded without mercy. This is exemplified by Providence himself out of the Garden cutting them down like sickness, and love is also the "jealous stepchild of God." Sekou appreciates the contradictions of love and would have his readers realize love is not always all that it is bruited to be. It is a tender plant needing careful nurture, or it can become a many-headed monster.

The monologues can be conveniently considered in this section on fiction. Two of them, "Great Grandmother 'T'" and "The Bad That Man and Woman Do," do not escape the all-pervading love theme. The matriarch's reference to her mother-in-law's love of light skin color is not unrelated to a comprehensive probing of the social geography of love. It also represents the culture of self-loathing identified in the poems. This contrasts with the view of Derio of a younger generation for whom black is beautiful although, if truth be told, the conventional philosophy still has contemporary currency. More central to the love theme, the issue of love and fidelity is depicted in the great grandmother's lover, who migrated "and come right back to me." Love is keeping one's word, she says in so many words.

It is perverted love in the form of immorality and debauchery that concerns the presenter in "The Bad That Man and Woman Do." Man is the arch-devil, puerile in his boast of his multiple love liaisons, and capable of incest, which must be the ultimate in venereal sins. It is refreshing to learn from the lips of a woman that her sex is not guiltless. Indeed, they are often their own worst enemies in the way they deride each other in telling "mens," "never never trust a woman becausin I know, I is one." The creole language underlines the worldly wisdom of an island girl. It is refreshing that although slavery is mentioned, it is not facilely blamed for every love-ill. The call is for unity among the sexes and social re-engineering in the form of education to "transform plantation mind and manners," which spell values. This is cooperative work.

> We are, here, now, together, from the thousands of years from which we are coming, knowing each other, janus-faced and Shango double-axe.

History is a motivator, but we must take responsibility for our future if we are to usher in new regimes of love.

Patriotism

It seemed sensible to position love of country at the end of the first chapter because it is this trait that drives Sekou's political thrust and fuels labor and liberation. This serious patriot begins with St. Martin and encompasses significant others. St. Martin is perhaps too small to contain this author's patriotic fervor. He is, after all, pan-Caribbean and Pan-African, even internationalist, in his outreach. It is difficult to isolate a Sekou volume that does not directly or obliquely reflect his unrepentant commitment to his country. Many a character ventriloquizes their creator's preoccupation, if not obsession, with love of roots. It may be Great Grandmother "T" reminiscing on "when me and all S'maatin was young" or the young woman in "The Bad That Man and Woman Do" affirming pride of place and staking her faith in local solutions: "We are, here, now, together."

The book *Born Here* is Sekou's first poetry collection published in St. Martin, two years after his return "home" in 1984. He had spent some 13 years of living, studying, and writing in the USA. The 1986 title is predicated on the affirmation of patriotism. Poems with titles like "Legacy," "Homeland Harvest," "A Nation Poem," "A First St. Maarten Poem," "Come Home," "Anthems," and even "On Caribbean Aesthetics" address the p-word more or less ostensibly. And "home" words and phrases such as "in our own land," "our way home," "born here," "our beloved country," and "this land of ours" liberally scattered in this single volume give manifold blazon of Sekou's patriotic ways. An ultimate aim is to make home an Eden of peace:

It is time for them, our Family
To Journey Home
To find the Eden Place of Peace.

The haunting rhythm heightens the emotional effect even though we are aware that peace is born of struggle. And in "Come Home," he says,

> It is time, Beloved Ones
> To find our way Home.

Home is not just St. Martin but home to a helpful and hopeful ideology of struggle for independence, a deeded home instead of "the backyard of the Hague house."[18] Fabian Badejo's comment on "Home" is relevant and insightful; it is an extended and an ideological home. "Home is political consciousness and cultural awareness; it is wherever people are in struggle, wherever freedom has not yet found abode, wherever it is just taking roots."[19] Sekou believes in the extended family, spanning even nations, and he has extended his patriotism correspondingly.

The poem "Love Majesty" from *Born Here* depicts lovely images of love, innocence, and beauty, but the poet finds it difficult to separate love of a woman personifying the island from a pulsing patriotism and his messianic purpose. To be "born a new day" is to generate a new St. Martin. Evidently a book like *National Symbols of St. Martin*, of which Sekou is editor and leading author, has patriotism written all over it; it is born out of patriotism with the prime aim of engendering and sustaining national consciousness and commitment in the present and succeeding generations. It is seminal and educative work, something from his heart and hand possessing power to live and serve the future hour. In his own words, "The labor and love, blood and tears, hopes and dreams of the St. Martin people have given birth to a national consciousness." He mobilizes like-minded patriots including influential publics to assist him. The book is inherently and ultimately "patriotic," concerned as it is with building a national identity among St. Martiners. *The Independence Papers* (1990) is cast in a similar mold. For Sekou, independence is a desirable end of patriotism.

There is a spiritual quality about coming home and those who do win the poet's favor. The coming home of Ademus in "The Wake" after sojourning in France, Cuba, and New York, even if it costs ultimately, makes him a true son. He is a pleasing contrast to those who swear that "they was never goin' back to S'maatin becausin ain nothing there." Sekou's patriotism and reverence for St. Martin is sometimes symbolized by salt—salt, which defines the island's history and deprivation. He is accordingly contemptuous of St. Martin folks who pass by with their children "without saluting the salt ponds of their foreparents' unreparated labor." And reverence is not enough. To love one's country is to fight for it, as "Plastic High" in *Images in the Yard* bears out. They lack patriotism who "Don't want to fight / For your own Mother / Land and all." With his typical deftness (one almost uses the archaic "sleight") of language, he draws attention to mother as in family, land, and also one's patria.

37 Poems, Sekou's most recent volume of poetry, also addresses the patriotism sub-theme not surprisingly in the "st. martin soul" poems. Unity and patriotism are conjoined like the twins to whom "st. martin soul I" is dedicated. To be raised in St. Martin is to love it, and all those who are raised there are bonded by that love: "When we raise up in it / when we raise it up / same.we.love.it so" and this love carries an obligation to give back to the country in a dialectical relationship. It may be subtler in "st. martin soul II," but the sense of rootedness is there. To be born and raised there is to be affected, shot through by its ambience and values, and you are committed to both its sweet and its salt. "The strainer," also in *37 Poems*, is more explicit; it is about nation building and ambition "to own they oan nation" where the double play on own/oan emphasizes "belongership" and ownership.

By extension patriotism includes love of Africa the real motherland. This can be illustrated from virtually anywhere in Sekou. On the surface, "Africanita" is about the love of a woman, but that woman is also Africa with whom the poet has a love affair. The opening couplet says so much about the geographical distance of Africa and at the same time the propinquity in blood.

I desire you more
For you are so close—yet so far.[20]

"This is Our Land" in *Maroon Lives* (1983) gets to the point. His target is not just apartheid, not just a superficial "sharing a bench / or shit-house with whites"—and an oppressive white minority at that. It is a tireless struggle for the commanding heights of power and for repossession of the land.

Sekou runs the gamut of the love theme, and this chapter does not claim to have treated his litany of love exhaustively. He merely alludes to love of family and children, for instance, recognizing that families are the sinews of the nation. In "st. martin children 1" of *37 Poems*, he aims at bastard motherlands

who from afar suffer the little children
to have them not to bigness come unto nation

and the line, "fight to be.long&love one another" is at once about love, children, and the sense of belonging. At the same time, children are a microcosm of the nation that must unite physically and spiritually (the sacramental images are so powerfully fresh) for such is the kingdom of St. Martin. His love of nature is evident in his imagery, ambience, and moods and his addictions to native, Caribbean color. This is an introduction to the epistle of love according to Sekou, to whom we give the last word—a felicitous word, an emotion-packed word of love and patriotism from *The Salt Reaper*:

> make us a world to
> call home.
> name it love.[21]

This word is of the ilk of the aphoristic:

> "see paris and die"
>
> . . .
>
> see st. martin and live
> all the reasons to.[22]

and the seduced reader says, "Amen."

2

LABOR

The Love-Labor Nexus

Sekou's national agenda for St. Martin recur throughout his work like the utterance of a Greek chorus, and the author has made the popular agenda his personal mission. The motivation for his mission is love—love for St. Martin, the Caribbean, and Africa as the case may be. It may appear incidental and unobtrusive, but the love-labor nexus is the deliberate crafting of a living philosophy.

The poem "For Summer Only" already cited in the preface is a clear statement of Sekou's mission and love and labor are conjoined. The critical lines for this chapter are

Let us go . . .
Into the streets
And love
Into the fields
And labor

In restating the agenda in *Brotherhood of the Spurs*, love-with-labor is again central, and Sekou universalizes the mission: "Man must know he is here to labor and lowe [*love*]. To battle for right and build that which is right."[1] In a long poem from *The Salt*

Reaper, pointedly titled "Cradle of the Nation," it appears again in the formula for liberation: "sun song and green rock of earth. / study.build. the soul.the science. / the love. the labor. the liberation." Love and labor define and give life to each other and purpose to life's endeavor.

Both love and labor are aspects of revolution, and the author's work as creative writer and artist is an aspect of his envisioned revolution. It is part of the labor of love. It certainly requires love to bear burdens and carry crosses and corpses, which are possible if not inevitable *en route* to revolution. After the counting of costs in "Love One Another," another poem from the contemplative *Images in the Yard*, he caps them with "Our love / And our Labor" as if these two actions were twinned. And when Napolina Gumbs, in a pithy evaluation in the preface to *Nativity and Monologues for Today* (1988), notes that the work "is a living culture of our collective labor, love and rites of liberation," she evidently has a true perception of Sekou's vision of labor.

In *Mothernation*, the yoking of love and labor takes on a different countenance. Labor in the common cause is a basis of love, and there is a romance in labor. In "to task," this is Sekou talking about his lover: "Like I told my love the other day / there are much hands to set about work / . . . / much land to till and tend." In "No Love Poems" from *The Salt Reaper*, he rejects love lyrics for the sake of lyrics and the Eurocentric mode and mold. Ironically, it is his love for St. Martin, its history, and its destiny that have given birth to this elegant poem of controlled emotion.

In his very first published volume, *Moods for Isis*, Sekou makes it clear that poetry is about love's labor. It begins to dawn on us even then that he is no dilettante as Taylor warns us. Making love is poetry in action, and writing poetry is birthing new consciousness. These lines are pregnant with meaning:

Althea Hill / Reminds me of a soul
Who knows of a poet / Traveling within her being
Who must be caught / And made love to . . .[2]

In his prose, Sekou puts beyond doubt his perception of the marriage of love and labor, if there were any. In his preface to *National Symbols of St. Martin*, he mentions love and labor first in a list of factors that combine to develop a national consciousness. In the pamphlet *Big Up St. Martin: Essay and Poem* (1999), he asserts that one mark of true leaders is that they "labor and love in fields with all the people." By linking love with labor, he ensures that the former is never a vacuous sentiment. This is perhaps the only time that labor precedes love in his treatment of the twin concepts. In fact, this short essay mentions love with labor no fewer than four times. First and very early in the essay, love and labor are treated as the energy and engine by which St. Martin people will build a Caribbean civilization as an increment to a better world. Making a similar claim, love and labor give direction to the people's striving.[3] They, among other things but they first and foremost, are consciously invested in nation building. The common Latin saying, *amor omnia vincit* (love conquers everything) is creatively and realistically extended in the title poem of *Nativity*: "Love and Labor Conquer All Things."[4]

Finally, the ultimate end of love and labor is political independence. Of this we are left in no doubt, for it is the closing sentence of the essay in *Big Up St. Martin*, the clinching thought as it were. Love and labor together are obviously critical to Sekou's philosophy of nation building. It is wrapped up in this final sentence: "Political independence must be realized by our very love and labor in order for democracy, equality, justice and prosperity to truly rise in St. Martin and prosper all of the nation's people."

Exploitative Labor

Sekou has never ceased to appeal to laborers, for work is absolutely necessary if liberation and independence are to be attained. This is readily supported by a couple lines in *37 Poems*: "'n' i'n never see a nation yet / build a country with ease and hardly without work."[5] Laziness has no place in Sekou's lexicon and philosophy. Once identified, a just cause must be pursued through love and labor. This is the tenor of "Triumphant Living" in *Maroon Lives*. The labor, however, must come from willing spirits who understand and share the purpose of their strivings. It must not be exploitative. This is why Sekou is an educator; he is not just conscripting people.

By the very method of recruitment, slave labor was iniquitous. No one has the words, phrases, and imagery to portray the disgust, humiliation, and nastiness of the slave triangle to match Sekou, and all within the realism and bounds of poetry. This is an area in which he speaks with a distinctive voice. In "Cradle of the Nation," one of his great poems, he perceives the European-to-African leg of the triangle as an invasion. Harpy-like, they "clawed in" material and human resources "from the gold coast&bays&bights, spitting fire mostly / to forage further, hinter, with the evil&greed&fear within."[6] The imagery of rapaciousness is evident, as is the inhumanity and beastly treatment in "rise and fall to the holds.the pens.the stock." And what pen but Sekou's can daub on paper the horrors and smells of the slave coast:

> wee crawled to the bucket of shit, fecal of the alone
> of the many

of all the heavens&hells
from coast to mountain boast.
lumped. dumped.
tumbled into the jaw-open pale stew of shit.
repository
stench.yard at goree:[7]

The barbs are equally sharp for the Middle Passage leading to slave labor. The story "A Salting" gives us an insight into the slave passage including the "baracoon waters" the dread repository. It seemed to the Africans an endless passage "through the middle of an underworld."[8] The storage and the stench were all part of the cruel rite of passage "to a new place, not of this world."[9] Their handlers certainly did not seem people of this normal world, certainly not like Sekou's romanticized Eden of altar thrones and gardens from which some of the Africans were kidnapped. Treatment on their arrival on the Caribbean labor coast was equally dehumanizing. They had to "feel-up" the goods including the teeth, "the handling of the cock and seeds of other men with coveting and leering and laughter."[10] The language may be abrasive to some but merely graphic to others, pitched as it is in a lexicon that common and not-so-common people understand. More importantly, it shows European greed and covetousness operating at different levels.

And don't expect Sekou's veneration for those metropolitan centers and their agents who came to plunder and wallow in the gutters of slavery. Turning their idiom of justification on its head, he dubs them "warring tribes" and associates them with a cold and hungry region and with being caught up in a dog-fight for human cargo, "clutching each other's throats / and shooting each other's balls out / walled up forts and wooden ships / coveting and conquering." Then there is this grasping greedy image:

... blood-ice claws
dunk and drag us here
chained and whipped
throw us up from stinking water-float maws.[11]

He is scathing, too, on the West Indian cricketers who celebrated apartheid in South Africa by playing there to the shame of blacks of goodwill everywhere. In these lines from "For 17 Cricketers" in *Born Here*, rhyme is used effectively to emphasize the pathos and heighten the hurt: "Look how they went there / to play a game / to shame all Africans."[12] Their lucrative "play" is a sad contrast to the tired old man in *Moods for Isis* whose labor was fruitless, thanks to his oppressors, the neoslave masters of his "continuing past."[13] The cricketers, however, were willing "slaves." Scorn is also poured on the rulers of Honduras for their oppressive administration; they are accused of:

"Throwing blood and shit and shame / On the name of their people."[14] Here he employs a similar literary device using rhyme as was identified in "For 17 Cricketers."

Slavery is not just exploitative; it is a perversion of labor for

... bitter work brought us here
hauled out and driven in like nails in palms and feet
from horrowful
mothership belly gutting out umbilical chains
severed
with vinegar salt and sea blood rust
lashed.[15]

and a kind of crucifixion as these images of cross and Christ suggest. Culture is work, but not after this sort. Child labor is insanely cruel and child slavery is doubly so. It is an interruption of a child's rhythm of life by inferior beings "who can not walk long in sunlight." In other words, only men of darkness and evil inflict this horror on members of the human race. Sekou is acutely aware that the enslaver is degraded and dehumanized in the very acting of enslaving other human beings. It produces a form of moral bankruptcy.

Sekou's vast (and I do mean vast) scholarship and thoughtful knowledge of St. Martin allow him to effectively delineate and define the horrors of chattel slavery. It is more than coerced labor on devil-white plantations under overseer whips where slaves toiled from dawn until dusk. And sugar plantation slavery was living death. We learn in "All Labor" from *Maroon Lives* that we toiled from morning not just in the fields but in the house. (The "we" is important because it registers Sekou's personal identification not only with the slaves but the oppressed everywhere.) Toiling in the house suggests more than just being a nonpraedial slave involving regular maid service. Toiling in the house suggests abuse and being caught up willy-nilly in the lecherous toils of the debauched planters and landlords. This is the ultimate in exploitative labor.

Religious collusion with slavery in which the Bible was another whip is held partly accountable for the attendant cruelty of labor. In *Quimbé – Poetics of sound* (1991), the poem "Preacherman" exposes the bankrupt religiosity of people "who kept slaves on their knees in church / on emancipation in 1800 & something." A hint of hypocrisy seems to reside in the juxtaposition of slave and church; but this was normal business in slavery. After all, there is hardly any irony in the fact that a good British ship called Jesus engaged in the slave trade. The kidnapped and enslaved ancestors were "hauled away in howling chains / in maws of gales of vessels, images / of the good ship jesus."[16] Slave labor had accomplices in high places, Sekou seems to say in the crafting of his pieces. No wonder slavery was hellish without impunity except that some of the labor, Sisyphus-like accomplished little, free labor being more productive and economical than slave labor.

Salt is St. Martin's sugar, and Sekou's intellectual equipment linked to his emotional involvement has produced some of the choicest imagery and description of the nightmare of slavery. Consider this powerful and graphic declaration of exploitation and waste in "Great Salt Pond Speaks" from *The Salt Reaper*: "I am the mudbag reservoir of your labor." Liverpool's introduction to the book says as much when he calls the salt ponds St. Martin's historical plantations. Red-blooded slavery was working in the salt ponds for the people of St. Martin, who reaped "pyramids of salt for the red white and blue / slave kingdoms."[17] Intentional or not, pyramids conjure up notions of Israelites building those structures under Egyptian bondage. The universality of slavery, whether it relates to Soweto or El Dorado, does not diminish its iniquity, and Sekou will inveigh against it even if he has to borrow the tongue of Cuban Nicolás Guillén.

The titling of a volume *The Salt Reaper* is a symbol of how deeply rooted in Sekou's consciousness is the exploitation that obtained in St. Martin. His people were treated like refuse as the salt ponds became their baptismal pool of cruelty. These lines with their accumulation of imageries of body waste say it all:

but you, now black as tar, would be
baptized in the pit of
salt
spit piss semen   & sweat. dumped. lumped.
lashed, raped, reviled&blooded.
The baptism was not just
the walk in
a lake of brine, mirror this splinter of.this crime of
centuries
drove you in like a nail in this wetland of salt
anointed[18]

In other words, slavery stinks. In "salt reaping I" and "salt reaping II" the work was hell, he says plainly. The poet tempers and controls his emotion by likening the work to lovemaking. Going down and in was sweet, but the outcome was so deceptive. There is controlled and cruel irony in this particular nexus of work and loving. The recurring comparison with Christ is there as he goes on to use words like "nail" and "palm" and "salt / anointed." Sekou may well be deliberately or subliminally implying that rightly discerned and rightly and positively "exploited" slave suffering and stolen labor can become redemptive. I believe this business of redemption is what this author is about. Clearly, this is one means by which he intends to honor the fallen among the cane and cotton fields, the mines, and the salt ponds. As Liverpool observes, he wishes to honor those who have worked since "it all had fall down so."[19]

Chika Unigwe, another reviewer of *The Salt Reaper* also recognizes that the title of the book connotes the St. Martin version of slavery in the salt mining work of the blacks of St. Martin. The reviewer illustrates the hardness of the labor by referring to the poem "salt reaping ii," from which we have quoted. In case we missed it, Unigwe draws attention to the disturbing parallel Sekou draws between arch-terrorist Osama bin Laden and those who have "been laden" with colonialism and neoimperialism and by implication with slavery. The poem under reference is "for/closure."

Slave labor did not end in 1800 and something, as Sekou would say. It has persisted into contemporary life in the form of neoslavery. The "poor who rummage in this rubbage"[20] of the Great Salt Pond; the "babies who now / walk through piles and pools of shit / to eat out food and mek a sale / from garbage dungle heaps / from egypt to mexico to pond dump"[21] are in a form of slavery, and it's more pernicious in the era of supposed freedom. This is why the voiceless need a voice to continuously evoke freedom, as is suggested in "Ages of Hunger" from *Images in the Yard*. Reinslavement is a real fear, especially for the youth of St. Martin. It may be even necessary to guard against the slave master's interpretation of Christianity, which many prefer as a workable alternative. It can terrorize the poor and serve as an "enemy of liberation," Sekou warns in *Images in the Yard*.[22] This may well contribute to underdevelopment; but he recognizes very early on that in the end the poor are poor because they do not work for themselves.[23] This is another reason for the drive to independence.

The seemingly harmless and lucrative tourist industry can be a major culprit. The casino worker of *Nativity* illustrates this. Managed as it is by expatriates from metropolitan countries no strangers to slavery, it can be exploitative. The repatriation of large profits from the strength of native labor if not properly managed can bear the marks of neoslavery. It may be a sensitive issue but if any one person provides insight into this economic hemorrhaging and the exploitation of the nation's resources, it is Sekou.

In "giving inches" from *The Salt Reaper*, he further questions whether the island exists for its people or for others. In so doing, he boldly questions the sacrosanctity of tourism. He is rightly critical of our written "panto" smile for visitors when set against our treatment of each other, including, one suspects, other Caribbean people. His potentially classic poem "double dutch.immigration at schiphol," which deals with humiliation of the black salt reaper in immigration, presents a marked contrast to the treatment which white and wealthy visitors receive in "friendly" Caribbean ports. The liberator must comprehensively diagnose his country's diseases, taking no symptoms for granted if he is to bring wholeness to the body politic.

Recognizing Sekou's interest in soil, seed and labor, I dedicated a poem to him in 1991, which reads in part

The Soil with Love
(For and After Lasana Sekou)

Yesterday we tilled the soil without love
Mama's labors lost like a miscarriage
the hungry earth sucked her blood
like a diablesse to bloat the master
Today we till the soil with laughter . . .

Labor for the National Cause

The necessity and dignity of labor are clearly articulated in "the strainer" from which we have already quoted. Although labor is not confined to agricultural work, Sekou pays considerable attention to farming apart from the rich metaphoric and symbolic meanings which he extracts from it. Typically, it was in plantation labor that slavery found its cruelest expression, and it is important to demonstrate that honest agricultural work is critical for sustained survival.

Sekou's revolutionary agenda have always included going "into the fields and labor"—as much as "a *revolución técnico* / and science to wuk up / the people's genius."[24] In *Moods for Isis* there are the lines "Let us sow another seed / That will bear abundant fruit" in "A Kwanza Poem," which operates on two levels. And *37 Poems*, the most recent volume, contains several pointed references to "The farmer, scythe, divined and destiny / in his right clay-worn hand,"[25] to heaves of grain and songs of the joy of harvest. The poem "Labor" in *Maroon Lives* is about farming, among other things. Labor is about sowing and reaping, and priests are invited (to put it mildly) to turn to planting. In manipulating imagery to make his point, Sekou is less concerned with any charge of being either irreligious or sacrilegious. Indeed he is happy to humanize Jesus when he wishes to invest ordinary people with revolutionary potential. He is accordingly against military police that forces a peasant farmer, "whose father could as well been a carpenter- / carry a heavy cross for four miles."[26] The reference to Jesus the Nazarine, the carpenter's son, is obvious, and the farmer father, who reappears in the poem "Liberation Theology," could also be Joseph or José next door.

Farming is critical to self-sufficiency and self-determination. Land is required not only for space to build and simply occupy but to "grow on." The allusion is from a poem in *Images in the Yard* significantly titled "Freedom Song." A country aspiring to independence must grow as much of its food as it can. For Sekou, the approach to liberation has to be at least two-fold. One must have plough shares and pruning hooks, while at the same time holding spears, whatever these are made of. "Let us grow corn and forge new spears,"[27] he admonishes in *For the Mighty Gods*. And in the *Moods for Isis* poem "Then," Sekou could well be wishing for the kind of agricultural program that will contribute to St. Martin's self-fulfillment. I believe this is captured in these lines of yearning:

And the midnight children
Shall rejoice even until daybreak
Where we will begin to labor
For our Self-fulfillment
In the fertile fields of our nation[28]

I am not unaware of the double if not treble meaning of the lines. In addition to the interest in agriculture as a development strategy in its own right, Sekou employs the sowing and planting metaphor frequently in his bid to galvanize wide support for his life's mission. Sowing is investment of human resources in anticipation of the bountiful harvest of liberation.

Very early in his poetic career Sekou uses the figure of sowing and reaping to underline the need for intellectual and emotional change of a fundamental nature as a prelude to independence, genuine nation building and human liberation. The sowing and reaping imagery also establishes the necessity for spade work and the investment of sweat and toil. "A Kwanza Poem" in the Love section of *Moods for Isis* contains these lines: "Let us again sow another seed / that will bear abundant fruit." The lines speak not of seminal planting, but the propagation of revolutionary ideas. *Images in the Yard* picks up the strain and explicitly connects sowing with revolt. Sustained poverty is itself a seed for revolution. Serious and elegant, these lines are worth a quote. Concerned over the wasted potential of children, he says:

Though we know
With work and time
That seeds of revolt
Are sown like this too / That Revolutions
Are also born of such seeming poverty[29]

Sekou makes two important observations in this context: Work is involved in fomenting revolution, and seeming inactivity should not be mistaken for pacification in a situation of social deprivation. This is the import of this one of his powerful one-liners, such as "That roots do not die in Winter." "Tribal Boundaries" in the same book, anticipates the harvest of revolution and the fall of Babylon: "We're coming through / Reaping- / For we sowed / Nations more numerous / Than the heads of the beast."[30] (Sekou should not be read superficially; the very positioning of the poems is significant. Sowing precedes reaping.) In *Mothernation*, Sekou likens political labor to sowing and reaping. In "working change" the newly enlightened emanate from plowed foreheads. This, too, is labor, as "wrinkled brows" further emphasizes. But there is beauty in this work: "to see the people work / cultivating the land / and making preparations for life."[31] In mothering a nation, education is important. This is also important labor and the employment of a pedagogy of liberation is another aspect of planting with a plug for science thrown in. So it is in "With Vision":

> It is our time
> to labor in a pedagogy of liberation / . . .
> for we are the generation planting the seeds and
> science / to harvest the Age of Fulfillment[32]

Labor is seamless and comprehensive embracing every discipline and all the willing. There is a sense of urgency to seize the strategic moment for "the sowing season is on hand / The land lays naked before us."[33] Not only is there anticipation of bountiful harvest, but "hallelujah" of *37 Poems* with its exultant rhythm conveys joyous anticipation as an oasis of victory springs between the rocks and deserts of the Antilles. There is excitement in the lines:

> you are the sun-stained harvest
> the bright calling voice
> the sudden field, a rousing flight
> the joyous yield
> between rock and desert[34]

Sekou needs this eternal optimism and freshness in this challenging, near-herculean task he has undertaken. The poem in itself brings vicarious and anticipatory pleasure. Thus, Sekou creates and dances to his own music as persons do in harvest: "Oh, the dance, the dance / The dawn crackling song bends." Emotion wells up and you want to hold your sides.

"Pleasure Divine" in *Moods for Isis* begins with the line, "Rich and fertile woman" in a poem about mutual sexual pleasure. And "fertile" is one of Sekou's favorite words, but he is more interested in the fertility that spawns political and revolutionary activity. When in *Born Here* he writes:

> Put your hands
> Between the legs of this island
> And bury seminal seeds
> For bountiful tomorrow[35]

the resultant progeny is revolutionary fervor, liberation, and democratic sentiment. If this were possible,
these lines from *Moods for Isis* quoted in chapter 1,
are even more explicit: "Freedom yearning eggs /
Actively waiting to be fertilized / By black warrior
sperm / So that a revolution may be conceived."[36] The
object of breeding is to produce warriors for the revolution. In these pieces, labor is construed as travailing
in the old sense of the word. It suggests strenuous
labor and even pain but the joy of producing a child
makes it bearable. In this sense, our author is forever
in labor. No sexist, Sekou is also interested in wom-
en warriors, provided they possess strength, beauty
and inquiring minds. These are they who give birth
"to stronger love / and better tomorrows."[37] On the
whole, the love act is not just liaison for pleasure but
a passion for reform. Innocence is not brooked. Roots
must be sown and earth watered for "Such innocence
/ Does not quench the thirst of this man."[38] Love and
procreation are also evident in "For Life" but whether
the partner is Africanita or *Antilleana dulce*, the aim
is to "bear fruit / into the twilight of life"[39] and these
are not flesh and blood children.

"The cubs are in the field" is predominantly about
labor and here, too, Sekou uses the sexual imagery
and graphically so. The cubs are not prepared to re-
treat

before the cock breaks the hymen of
spread-legged dawn
inviting us to lick open destiny's lips to orgasmic sight
to see for true where the word to be made flesh
comes from . . .[40]

"Cock" apart, the felicitous overlay of religious imagery works well with its suggestion of new dawn, new birth, and new destiny, not to mention the messianic notion of the word made flesh. This is one of those Sekou moments of magic.

After educating the people in "Colony, Territory, or Partners?" Sekou concludes that democracy, equality, justice, prosperity, and political independence can only come through love and labor. This must be cooperative labor in which leaders have led to combine energies. For "true leaders will labor and love in the fields with all of the people."[41] So leaders who do not attain to this standard are pilloried. These undeveloped rulers are dismissed as cowardly, "hiding in quilted pampers / babbling diabolical baby talk."[42] Leadership, he suggests, is not for pueriles; and whether it is in the field or in the house, including the House of Parliament, labor is involved. He is equally dismissive of spectators who may well be either cowards or traitors. This is the import of "Data" in *For the Mighty Gods*. The call is for doers and not bystanders. Equally, those who are sowing false seeds must be eliminated even if it takes new blood and a new breed to do so. For the approved midwives are rowing out to sea and in

> Only a matter of hours / and we workers here-
> Borning new tides / And carrying the lives
> Of those who died
> While waging our Victory-
> Will chase the fascists farmers
> From our Beloved Country[43]

Details are important in Sekou, and one finds the word "tides" significant. It is not just new tidings but new waves and currents, indeed a new philosophy that will underpin the political thrust.

I have already hinted that the Sekou workforce includes more than just scientists, political agitators, or well-schooled career politicians. Media persons, and artists are workers, too, and need to come on board. *The Independence Papers* provides us with some insight and the curriculum for independence. The mass media must not be politically manipulated, and their ideology must be acceptable to the masses. They should, like *Newsday*, figure in the social transformation of St. Martin. Even so, Sekou calls for more progressive content, analyses, and content which reflect popular ideas and views on critical issues such as independence. More to the point, they must educate workers and expose exploitation; and Sekou endorses

L.A. Perez, Jr.'s critical view of the tourist industry:

> Insofar as tourism is an economic activity directed by and organized for metropolitan interests, the travel industry has accomplished little to alter basic relationships rooted in the colonial past.[44]

Astute enough to realize that the pro-independence media can in turn be charged with manipulation and propagandizing, he recommends a genuine ideology of neutrality and objectivity. This does not prevent particular newspapers from helping to set a progressive national agenda in preparation for independence. Even if press objectivity is in many cases largely theoretical, it is important for Sekou to take that stance. This gives him a moral platform from which to attack the "free / And objective American press" for misinforming the world on the real goals of their assault on Grenada and Lebanon. The reference is to "Propaganda" in *Maroon Lives*, and Sekou obviously wishes to differentiate between his kind of progressive propaganda and the fallacious type, which the dominant western media presumably pursues. One suspects also that the St. Martin media will need to assist the people in the unlearning process to undo the harm which "Their misinformation media" have done rewriting history to cement imperial sway and culture.[45] The media certainly has a remedial and damage control role.

Artists and cultural workers must also keep independence in the public domain and must generally be responsive and sensitive to social issues. In Sekou's aphoristic words: "A true people's art is dynamic, not dogmatic. It is fresh not fearful"; and for him, Arts must help to "seed this new beginning for St. Maarten."[46] That word "seed" with which we are now very familiar gives us a strong clue to the mission of the artist. "Fearful" is also a critical word because the revolutionary artists modeled on Sekou become a target for counter-revolutionary forces. It is intriguing that Sekou wishes the artists to respond to critics from the standpoint of the rightness of their cause. The question arises: Are they always right? This is important because the true artist is not supposed to be "dogmatic." He is rather less proper in "Nativity" where the Br'er patches and Derek Walcott's Ti-jean as Anansi (the legendary trickster spider) are expected to overthrow devil-white plantation and overseer-with-whip "by any means necessary."[47]

Sekou is well aware of the progressive and ideological role of artists like Kamau Brathwaite, Aimé Césaire, George Lamming, Linton Kwesi Johnson, Frantz Fanon, Bob Marley, Mickey Smith and others. He is also aware of their potential revolutionary function, and they provide him with inspiration. He himself is, however, one of the most impressive of a poet/artist whose pen is an instrument of agitation and revolution. In that sense his poetry is labor, too.

One does not have to read between the lines. Sekou is conscious of the purpose of his poetry. In some often-quoted lines from *The Salt Reaper*, he differentiates between "pleasant sing-songs" and revolutionary poetry:

There will be no love poems tonight
>   only sweaty words
>   pond salt rhymes
>   calloused complaints from people's voices
>   oral, alive, a salve, conscious, lyrics
to rub on each other's bruised, whipped backs.[48]

We have here a working insight into his poetic agenda. "Pond salt" situates the work in St. Martin; and for a start, he inveighs against neoslavery and be the voice of the voiceless, or the inarticulate. This claim can be illustrated throughout the length and breadth of Sekou's work, and even some of his love poems harbor serious political undertones. Thus, Liverpool is correct when he observes in his erudite introduction to this same volume that: "His poems thus underscore a restlessness . . . and an idealism that are bases of many a revolutionary."

The early poem "P.O.W. (Poets of War)" in *Moods for Isis* is self-evident, and the poet is self-designated. As a poet, he labors to unmask lies and search for truth. Sekou is not as innocent as he claims in the line "For I call upon the name of peace progress and Allah." He does more:

> For I told the young flowers
> To piss their metabolic waste
> Upon the un-holy sanctu
> aries.

I agree that Sekou is a poet of war and that without condemnation. In these still colonial territories, art for art's sake is a luxury we cannot afford all of the time. For Sekou, poets are absolutely essential to life; they not only sing of beauty but also "curse the demons of evil." He labors more diligently at the latter because that is what the season demands. In spite of the imagery of righteous anger, this action too is a labor of love.

Part of the labor lies in the performance of his poetry, and the performance element is in part crafted into the pieces. This is what Khair says eloquently in the introduction to *37 Poems*: "Sekou inflects his poems with oral rhythms but also with literary and chirographic (visual) experimentation." The point is worth belaboring that performance is never about entertainment merely but a palatable and engaging way of getting his message across. The performances are mixtures of celebration and cerebration, of theater and scholarship.

LIBERATION

Liberating the Mighty

In early August 2005, the St. Martin media published an article in which Sekou reiterated the avenues to success as "a compound of constant working solutions: love, labor, liberation." All of these are at work simultaneously, continuously reinforcing each other, so it is logical to deal with liberation in this third chapter because in a sense, the other two are prologues, albeit substantial prologues, to the supreme theme and goal of liberation. The ends of the lifelong mission are emancipation and independence for St. Martin not forgetting the pan-Caribbean and global dimensions.

Situations exist in St. Martin to be set right. Divided and owned by two European countries, the island is doubly disadvantaged; in Sekou's eyes St. Martin's colonialism is not particularly benevolent. One of his aims is a genuine participatory democracy along with decolonization and Caribbeanization of his "homeland." The tourist trade is an example of another area in need of liberation; it is about ownership. In the ironically titled "Friendly Island" in *Born Here*, we work "In other people's hotels and stores and offices / Treat each other rough / Like hogs and cows" while reserving the "winter panto" smile for the tourist. Ownership is a critical issue with Sekou. The waves of independence are expected to inundate this neoimperial humbug.

The author's consistency of purpose is borne out by the fact that these concerns are presented with cogency, freshness, and enthusiasm in *The Salt Reaper*, half of which was written in the twenty-first century; and the political orientation and engagement are also evident in *37 Poems* of 2005. Following "No Love Poems," which opens the former, "The Blockade Next Time," which was inspired by the St. Martin protest of January 15, 1990, articulates Sekou's no-nonsense posture and something of the agenda of liberation. As I shall emphasize later, he understood well the cost of liberation.

Liberation must be addressed on several fronts; leaders, people, children, opinion leaders, and social shakers have a stake and a role. Leaders can be part of the impedimenta and must be reformed or be removed if they are mere lackeys and surrogates of the metropolitan administration or imperialists. The leaders must garner the will of the people off a democratic fashion. So the call is for "new law-givers of just statutes / of consensus gatherings." Sekou reserves the most revolting and contemptuous imagery for rulers. In "Downpression," also in *Born Here*, rulers nest with foreign chickens and extract withal a stink that infects duty's entire body politic. As a result, there is a dereliction of duty and "Boils all over the people / Pus running over the face of the land." Sekou apportions blame with the fearlessness of the liberator; he castigates rulers as too bleached in winter's whiteness, which betrays their orientation and perspectives. And oh the incongruity, the mismatch and the disconnect of "We wear winter woven culture / In tropic streets."

"Pretty punks" and the liberally used "parasites" are some of the self-explanatory imageries used; when "paternal" precedes parasites, the reference is to the metropolitan overlords. "The sleeping senator 'n dem" are more harmful for being harmless, especially when in their drowsiness they merely make excuses for the colonizers. It angers the poet that these same councilors will seek reelection with lying promises feeling up the people's emotion. "Feel up" attached to charlatan politicians is such a delicious imagery of political seduction. Liberation has to also begin in high places. Sekou is equally critical of rulers elsewhere who are gross and manipulable. He empathizes with the black poor of Haiti who must tolerate "fat/peanut brained rulers" who "dangle from a puppet's hanging chain."[1] Politicians apart, other authority figures are also regarded as obstacles to freedom. In "The Sick Generals" from *For the Mighty Gods*, these are attacked with the use of despicable images. Those who rob wealth from the land are dismissed as "leprous dogs" and "rapid dogs," for instance. Generally, it is accepted as given that there are wrongs to be righted. This necessarily involves casting down the wicked in high places and those "sitting in the seats of judgement."[2]

Speaking of high places, St. Martin, and by extension the Caribbean, needs to be liberated from uncritical religiosity. Sekou is scarcely more reverent in dealing with church leaders, the Pope included, than with political leaders except that with the former he makes more use of irony which is more deadly for being polite. A supreme example of mocking irony is connected with a pope's visit to the Dominican Republic, which was expected to cost the government five million US dollars "To protect him." Then comes the devastating double meaning of "I believe in God / But that is not right."[3] The poem "Rev Lie" from *Images in the Yard* is more patently brutal and would not endear the poet to orthodox Christians. He accuses preachers of being in cahoots with slave masters "hiding in luxurious cloth / Sharing in the rape of the poor and ignorant." These are serious charges that cannot apply equally to all men of the cloth, but Liverpool has warned that Sekou is uncomfortable reading and this applies perhaps even more so to preachers whose religion does not ameliorate the human condition and whose God is etherial or cross-bound:

> Take your god
> Liberate him from the bloody cross . . .
> Let him fight for the right . . .
> And let him walk
> Among mortal men

He is liberating not just the mighty but the Almighty.

Sekou's poem is hopefully part of the redemptive work for preachers and, yes, their gods. It is not that the author is a blatant unbeliever, but his faith is reserved for a God made in his own revolutionary image. The title poem in *For the Mighty Gods* describes his kind of god. He must be one who reeducates the people, conspires against the enemy, inspires awesome love songs, urges just wars, and be of the ilk of his assortment of icons and heroes most of whom are Africans and Caribbean persons. Essentially, he allows for the creation of man's own gods, which places him at odds with the dictates of the Judeo-Christian god. Even the most devout Christian is given something to think about and "reasoning," in the Rastafarian sense, is a healthy precursor to genuine liberation.

Liberation of the People

Given the kind of indoctrination and acculturation to which the people have been exposed, their liberation is an imperative. We have already discussed Christianity as a stronghold (Sekou would perhaps prefer stranglehold) and its hold on the people of St. Martin and the Caribbean. One suspects Sekou has an uphill battle to reduce the influence of traditional religion, but he approaches the task with alacrity and all the literary tools in his armory. Sekou is aware that the Christian tenet of a future paradise can dull the edge of activity to radically improve the conditions of this present life and produce bankrupt pacifists instead. This in part is the burden of "Blame Victims," which plainly and positively states,

That paradise
As anything good
As a living right
Must be fought for
Here
On this Earth[4]

The acceptance of this ideology is basic for revolutionary activity: the realization that there is no pie in the sky. Note the isolated power of "Here." Heaven, according to Sekou, is likened to a kind of terrorism that paralyzes the poor

With helpless images of redemption

To be found in far off places[5]

The line, "Must be fought for" is critical, because in Sekou's theology the meek do not automatically inherit the earth. Struggle of some kind is imperative. "Agenda" from the same volume is explicit. The people will only come into their own "Fighting for Rights by all means necessary." To fail to fight, for instance, is to settle for

sharing a bench
or shit-house with whites

in apartheid South Africa. The relevant poem in *Maroon Lives* ends with the line: "We fight on." Sekou is no open and explicit advocate of violence and he treats knowledge as a weapon. However, a phrase such as "by all means necessary" begs the question; and still in *Maroon Lives*, in memorializing Michael Smith he produces these significant lines which contain some possible means of the revolutionary struggle:

Every time one drops
A thousand more done rise
        armed with knowledge and time
            with arms and sight[6]

So he does not rule out much including "the jaw bone of an ass."

The tendency to collude with strangers against one's own and the shabby treatment of blacks are twin scourges that come under the fire of the liberator. One claim is that after our poor and deprived parents literally did the groundwork, strangers have infiltrated the country to suck the sweets and to cumulatively mar our destiny by introducing new ideas to our children. The greater unease of Sekou is that these immigrant *diablesses* are in bed with local judases. Those who thus sell their self-respect stand in need of liberation. (The *diablesse* of course is just another parasite in supernatural dress.) It is Sekou's thesis that the black man will only begin to receive respectable treatment without profiling, especially when he travels, after renewal; and the shift must begin at home. It will not happen, he says in *The Salt Reaper* "till when he enters his familyfull word to manifold flesh / to anew civilization."[7] A new dispensation is implied here. This is what will change the schiphol experience[8] with its modern apartheid when the nonwhite traveler was told, "sit, marked man" with the help of dog and gun.

Mimicry and a psychology of dependence are conditions of colonial conditioning, so the decolonization process has to address these. Antidotes to mimicry have to include self-acceptance and self-affirmation and the hackneyed saying, "black is beautiful" is very relevant. Sekou's affection for and affinity with Rastafarians is not a matter of fashion. Their "I

& I" values and locks of truth on their heads link them firmly with the African past and make them important in the business of self-definition. The maroons, too, who resisted slavery, add their own ingredient to black pride and black self-actualization, which is at the top of the famous Maslow's hierarchy of needs.

If black pride is to be entrenched and this is not unrelated to independence, self-deceiving blacks need to be liberated from "hating self for being so Black"; they must come to accept that

tight&loose
curled
hair
&
full
lips
kisssweet.[9]

Josette, an approved lover in the story "New Year's Eve Born," has not unsurprisingly abandoned frying her hair. In other words, she symbolizes what is natural, indigenous, and whole in St. Martin in contrast to those who strive for white characteristics. Josette is not the type to be "Hiding our behind in designer jeans / Flattening our African form / In cheaply European conforms." She would not be molded into an "allwhitey" image.[10]

Sekou's promotion of folk life and customs is part

of the process of building a culture of liberation by respecting and valuing what is local or of the nation or region over what is foreign. When in the short story, "The Wake," Ademus poured a few sips of Miss Ruby's fine guavaberry in the center of the grounding, this is a mark of respect for the national drink and for dead ancestors. Generally, Sekou's poetry and prose celebrate the life of folk, their loves, their food, their music, their herbal remedies (such as boiled breadfruit leaf drink for diabetes), their superstition, their wisdom such as that of Stupidy Nora in "The Rightful Heirs," and their language. When in the "The Wake" Cyus says, "they say when a man lowe too much it is that woman who goin' betray him. Oi doan know if it is so 'causin Oi lowe a whole lot but that woman of moine is an angel sen' straight from The Holy Father," the author is not just sustaining realism. He is giving creole language equal status with standard English as a valid medium of communication. This is as politically functional as rooting figurative language in local or national life. So the line "truth is a fat sweet mango" is about self-affirmation, too, and is therefore foundational for liberation.

Mimicry is allied to a spirit of dependence, and obviously that spirit is antithetical to the thrust for an independent St. Martin. This dependency dubbed as "drunken" is alluded to in *Maroon Lives*.[11] It is like "supping the master's waste"; it is cricketers lapping shit in South Africa giving a chance to the suppressor to abort the revolution. The dependency is manifested when we allow the neocolonizer (and not to forget the self-loather), "to dope us / withlightnesscomplexionoffairskindednessandslopoff / aboutallthatgoodhairstuffedupstuff."[12] In other words, when we allow persons and systems peddling European or white chauvinism to indoctrinate us with their ideal of beauty, and we allow others to define us, by "mimicking their pale styles." (The last quotation is from the intriguingly titled "The Hasbeenlicktuals" in *Images in the Yard*.) These lines from *Born Here* are irresistible in the case for black beauty and self-affirmation:

Our nose
Was so lovingly spread and sculptured
In that first tender moment of creation
And our lips
For being so fully grown.[13]

We should not, therefore, succumb to Aryan arrogance and alien definitions. If looking for designations for Lasana M. Sekou, one could comfortably add poet of negritude *par excellence*. The condition described here needs quality liberation not provided by missionaries; it needs self-liberation as emphasized in *For the Mighty Gods*. It is by our own liberating efforts (and again, "by any means necessary") that we return to self-destiny[14]; and Sekou is convinced that people fighting for Self will conquer whether in Vietnam or St. Martin. We hope he is right.

The act of liberation will cost. Of this Sekou is under no illusion, as we glean from some of his pieces. This quotation in *Maroon Lives* from Walter Rodney makes the unquestioned point, albeit with a sad prophetic irony:

> It is true that at times in a revolution blood flows. Very often innocent blood, very often the blood of the best among us. But one must be prepared to take a stand among evil and injustice in society.[15]

This, however, must not stop reformers from "trodding in unto upful tomorrows."[16] References to cross, blood, and Jesus suggest sacrifice and death; but there is a suggestion that death can be redemptive. In the poem "For Walter Rodney" we are told,

> We have come this far
> *Seen*
> In the Blood of our fallen fighters
> In our forwarding freedom
> . . .
> We are risen[17]

And in "For Michael Smith" also in *Maroon Lives* it is evident that the dreamer can be killed. It is clear that Sekou has thought deeply about this liberation business, and one suspects that he knows that there are subtle ways of killing a Joseph, even if short of physical death.

Models for Liberalizing Action

Although Sekou's acute focus is the liberation of St. Martin, his vision is global. It is not surprising therefore that he globe-trots to identify precursors and models for inspiration and affirmation. His pages on revolutionaries breathe the spirit of solidarity. One would hope that Sekou and his posse would learn from the mistakes of his forebears and not be condemned to repeat them. Sekou is not just examining models; he is part of the crowd of witnesses cheering and pronouncing judgement on wicked rulers and counter-revolutionaries.

Sekou is a great admirer of Maurice Bishop, who was not building just another society "but a just society"—a cause he espouses for his own St. Martin. He rightly blames the counter-revolutionary action of the US and their abiding big-stick policies but is not silent either on ideological differences in the Bishop ranks. He urged the Grenadians to fight in the spirit of Fedon and Fanon and numbers Bishop among his heroes of truth and strength, "And / Jacqueline Creft / who left so soon."[18] There is empathy, pathos, and warm emotion in the rhythm of these lines. He also recognizes traitors in the Caribbean ranks and attacks them savagely, whether it is Eugenia Charles or "Peeping" Tom Adams "using Barbados airport for enemies."[19] Sekou provides us with an impressive roll call of heroes in,[20] but one would wish to give some of them only critical endorsement.

It is worth emphasizing that Sekou took special interest in the thwarting of Grenada Revolution in 1983 and in Bishop, its prime protagonist. From front to back cover, *Maroon Lives* is dedicated to that cause the author so passionately espoused. The success of this revolution would have been for him an opening skirmish and microcosm of a globalized liberation of oppressed people everywhere from under the iron heals of neoimperialists. His depth of disappointment and anger at its failure are expressed in the most damning and dismissive imagery and epithets of loathing in naming and shaming the forces of the invasion and their Caribbean accomplices. There is very little nicety of irony in his "execratory tone."[21] In "War Dogs," they sup their "master's waste"; in "Drink Water Children," they are "dogs"; in "Maroon Lives," they are the "Babylonian whore"; and the colluding Caribbean states are "baying jackals."[22]

Eternal optimist with unquenchable revolutionary fervor, Sekou will not be cowed into defeat, he convinces himself and us, perhaps. The invasion is not the last word, for "We will speak again,"[23] and "We will cast them down."[24] Even if a somber aura dulls the hope and enthusiasm of these lines, the two poems "We Continue" and "Continuum" shore up resolve. They breathe the tone of resolution, which emanates from Martin Carter's "University of Hunger" in these lines: "O long is the march of men and long is the life / and wide is the span." For Sekou, the flame of liberty is eternal, and the struggle is like a living organism that refuses to die. "Continuum" recognizes that the route to revolution is long and a continuum suggests varied experiences *en route*, including losing battles but with prospects to ultimately win the war. A divided (remember, divide and rule) Caribbean was one of the shoals on which the Bishop's ship of revolution foundered. In *Maroon Lives*, Sekou rallies the family, the comrades, and *compañeros*, for revolution requires united action of persons of like history and culture. So we

Unleash our tongues from isolation/
Speak our destiny
As we fight for liberation.
In solidarity
Speak of destiny.[25]

For him liberation aborted is not destiny denied. He has learned this and other lessons from the Grenada debacle for investment in his own revolutionary agenda. The book *Maroon Lives* is part of the weapon, for his art is a tool of liberation.

Haiti, which has suffered from multiple interventions by the US and the regional country most in need of liberation, receives much attention. Coupled with Cuba, it is important for demonstrating that metropolitan powers can be beaten. The current task is to free it from the neoimperialists who are harbingers of "democrazy" and poverty with the mocking impact of the juxtaposition.[26] *The Salt Reaper* devotes a number of poems to Haiti or the Haitian condition. He applies the word fellowship in "Visit&Fellowship I" in two senses: as study and as solidarity in common cause with Haiti, which needs liberation. "Visit &Fellowship II" is also relevant to Haiti, which, like the Dominican Republic, was a victim of US imperialism underpinned by the pernicious and high-handed "ideology" of Manifest Destiny. Freedom and "holy democracy" will only come through "sweat&sacrifice &study&science." The implication is that these same tools of liberation are applicable to St. Martin. In the poem "Haiti 200," Haiti is the punished victor *vis-à-vis* neoimperialism, depicted with unsavory imagery: "... a serpent, ashen white in sunlight grave&grin / with a coffin in its mouth." Elsewhere, the evils of the Duvaliers as fleecing dictatorial leaders get the thumbs-down. In 1983, Sekou called on Haitian youths to rise up against Baby Doc and drive him from the blood-drenched palace.[27] In this at least, Haiti was successful, but without a secure future.

South and Central America combine an obvious province of strongmen. In "The Greatest March" from *Maroon Lives*, Sekou catalogs the ills of rulers in Argentina, and in Nicaragua and Honduras, both of which obtained independence from Spain in 1821. Freedom fighters in those countries should overthrow them for, among other things, "Throwing blood & shit & shame / On the name of their people." This gives the poet another opportunity to use that internal rhyme so effectively for emphasis. It also gives him a chance to mount one of his famous hobbyhorses: the irrelevance of the church to the struggle, for Pope John Paul brought nothing but "Papal Bull / & no food." This is a brutal wake-up call for the church. US President Ronald Reagan is dismissed as a senile gunman for colluding with the Samoza regime, but Sekou expects the programs of land reform and popular education to succeed. El Salvador and Namibia were waiting in the wings to join "the great march," which included Grenada, Cuba, and presumably St. Martin, as the poet sees it. People power is highlighted in this poem, and "the sowing season is at hand." Iraq of British and US "occupation" does not escape notice given what he would perceive as near-parallel situations in the Caribbean. Indeed, the St. Martin experience is regarded as occupation of sorts being the other gulf "where even the clouds are gray today."[28] Lisa Allen-Agostini insightfully draws comparison with Guadeloupe, Puerto Rico, and Aruba his birthplace where moves for independence are stymied by economic benefits resident in colonialism.[29] The Iraq poems in *37 Poems* allows him to attack militarism and invasion and the news hype of the conflict. Negative models inspire too, if only by generating, controlled rage.

Sekou takes special interest in Africa, "our land" whether it is Namibia or apartheid South Africa. In the spirit of Pan-Africanism, he expressed solidarity with South Africa and saw the issue not as civil rights but as African ownership. It is a fight for life and a rejection of any other claim of divine rights to divide an African country.[30] To build the liberation on solid foundations, he advised young Africans to educate themselves in their history. They can extract inspiration from the knowledge that

> My Zulu Impis, with shield and assagai
> Defeated 2000 British troops, with guns and cannons
> At the Battle of Isandlhwana
> Where the last Napoleon fell
> To the death of his family's blood-line[31]

Part of Sekou's own power lies in his profound

knowledge of history. History would have helped young South Africans to have a true perspective of those white South Africans upholding apartheid who were the real barbarians selling "democrazy."[32] Zimbabwe's Robert Mugabe is hailed by Sekou in 1986 in "Overstanding." Given the latter's mindset, including his democratic sentiment, that leader's recent predicament *vis-à-vis* the country's political climate and media restrictions would not be met with the approval of Sekou, but his expropriation program may well win the warrior-poet's approval, dubious as this may be in the minds of some.

In addition to a Mugabe, a number of personalities appear in a number of poems as icons and messiahs and are therefore potential models or at least kindred spirits. Prominent among these are Jean-Bertrand Aristide, "Che" Guevara, Fidel Castro, C.L.R. James, Marcus Garvey, Paulo Freire, Ho Chi Mihn, Nelson Mandela, Maurice Bishop, Bob Marley, Kamau Brathwaite, George Lamming, Lilian Ngoyi, Walter Rodney, and Jacqueline Creft. He even adds a Palestine Liberation Organization warrior and a South West Africa People's Organization fighter, and he is a great admirer of the Rastafarians whose diction he uses liberally in his work and also in his life—these brothers of "upful greetings" and "overstanding."

This is a somewhat disparate group: some have in

common socialist or left-of-center politics, some are merely stridently anti-imperialist and anti-American in particular, some are radicals in a positive sense, some are populist thinkers and workers, and some are artists with a revolutionary edge to their work. The common factor, one suspects, is the element of resistance that links them to Sekou.

One hesitates to label Sekou socialist or even pragmatist or to tie him down to any *ism*, but he is at least *progressive*, whatever that means. Anyone in these colonized spaces rooting for independence and meaningful democratization cannot be conservative, and he or she cannot support the status quo; therefore, he or she becomes a marked person. Thus, it suits Sekou's purpose to gather all these persons around him ideologically and be eclectic, extracting from each what he thinks necessary to build a new political culture, a new synthesis for St. Martin.

It is still my contention, however, that Sekou may need to be more critical of his heroes lest he merely changes the color of tyranny. Cubans still vote by boat against Castro, and some sovereign English-speaking Caribbean states have exchanged Britain for the World Bank and International Monetary Fund (IMF), which consist of the powerful metropolitan countries in another dress. I believe Allen-Agostini is sounding a similar warning when she questions, "Is sovereignty all it's cracked up to be when corruption, inefficiency, and shockingly fragile economies seem to be the fruit of that labor?"[33] That said, continuing colonialism cannot be an option in the twenty-first century, and Sekou need not feel daunted. He correctly takes as a given that political independence remains the time-tested, unavoidable, and necessary first step to the true and widest possible social and material development for the individual and democracy and prosperity for the nation.[34] However, some Caribbean independent states are not as prosperous as he suggests—and in titles between 1986 and 2005, he seems well aware of the challenges of independence in poems such as "In Transit," "caracas," "in trinidad," "movements," and "the blood boil." The point is, Sekou must ensure that his model is informed by any well-meaning criticisms his seductive art and fertile intellect may have attracted.

Speaking of a model for independence, how can his ideal omit Garvey's thrust for black economic enterprise and pride in blackness? It does not. He is bound to admire Castro's positive work in education and medicine in Cuba and the fact that he has been able to stave off the giant of the north, to the chagrin of the latter, for half a century. Inevitably, he also will recognize the affinity between the educative and "conscientization" work of Freire and his own humanizing agenda. And which comprehensive reformer can ignore the palatable radicalism of Marley, Brathwaite, Lamming, and company, men after Sekou's own heart? There is a revolutionary fervor and commitment resident in many of the named political activists. Sekou has the analytical tools and practical wisdom to critically and wisely use all the sources available to him. Against that background, his liberation agenda can stand the test of time.

Consonant with Sekou's mentality and his reverence for ancestral wisdom, home-grown heroes are not excluded from his scroll of honor. Prominent among them is José Lake, Sr. who, writing in his *Windward Islands Opinion*, agitated for independence in the mid-1960s.[35] He was a man after Sekou's heart and gives pedigree to the liberation struggle. A persecuted patriot, he is profiled for national reading in *National Symbols of St. Martin* where he is described as "beloved son of the soil," "freedom fighter," "labor organizer," and "orator." He features in several poems with the *Opinion* motto, "Love and Labor Conquer All Things" put in his mouth in "Nativity" and he is sandwiched between Rodney and Mahatma in "Overstanding." In the *Born Here* poem significantly titled "Legacy," he is "Father of the fighting word / Dean of the political sword" and all the more precious for being from "right here." Sekou warns against saints and hypocrites, but saints have a voice too, as Sekou readily admits by including the counsel of Martin Luther King, Jr. and Malcolm X. Garveyite Thomas Emanuel Duruo, also profiled in the national symbols primer, espoused the unity of St. Martin, an issue dear to Sekou's spirit. A poem entitled with his name in *Born Here* proclaims him a freedom fighter and decolonizer through his anti-plantation preachings. He sowed seeds that Sekou and others coming after will reap.

Joseph Lake, Jr., the poet's brother, who, according to Badejo, is "well known for his powerful, pulpit-like public addresses,"[36] is eulogized in the *Mothernation* poem titled "Joseph." Like his father before him, he has attracted enemies having been "scalped / by the unholy flames of their thorned tongues." Fiery trials would only serve to make him stronger and still firm on the vanguard of the revolution. With a grandfather in Duruo, a father in José Lake, Sr. and a brother in Joseph, Sekou emanated from a powerful pedigree of prophets and orators and could not escape the same heroic destiny. If anything, he embodies the quintessential qualities of political philosopher and would-be liberator partly as a result of this legacy. Like Shakespeare's Hamlet, he was born to set things right, and for him this is a welcomed, not a cursed, spite. His philosophy of liberation is rooted in a rich ancestral tradition.

This tradition includes the Maroons, who get a book title and are given a prominent page in the island's history. *National Symbols of St. Martin* describes these runaway slaves as "brave freedom-loving Africans" whose activities "were the most militant and independent manifestation of the fight for freedom."[37] *Marronage* is an Americas-wide phenomenon with Jamaica as its Caribbean headquarters, as it were. But it existed in St. Martin, thereby providing Sekou with liberation forerunners in his own history. He is walking proudly in the path that the maroons literally and figuratively trod; his work parallels theirs in its focus on liberation and nationhood.

Revolts and revolutions as recorded in history are important because they reveal resistance and a culture of rejection of tame submission to oppression. So in Sekou's work, the Morant Bay rising of 1865 in Jamaica is important, as are slave revolts such as Mackandal's in Santo Domingo, Fedon's in Grenada, and Bussa's in Barbados. The universal quest for freedom is emphasized with reference to resistance movements further afield such as the Nat Turner's rebellion in Virginia and the Tiananmen saga in China where curiously, and perhaps as a mark of his disgust at the outcome, "i forsook the forbidden city / for a perfect set of eyes."[38] Persons like Che Guevara the arch-revolutionary of Argentina, José Martí, and Castro of Cuba are particularly revered, warts and all, and Sekou is not particularly keen on focusing on the warts of his high-priestly heroes. Maroon exploits of course whether in Brazil, Surinam, St. Vincent, Jamaica with Nanny, and in St. Martin with the Diamond Estate runaways are celebrated.

Finally, in the post-emancipation era democratic developments such as trade unionism, which give the people a voice at the workplace and elsewhere, feature in Sekou's cultural resources. Uriah "Buzz" Butler is even dearer to his heart because trade unionism is in his personal heritage through his father, labor organizer Lake, Sr. When one considers the entire cavalcade of persons, personalities, revolutionaries, and freedom fighters (designate them how you will), one becomes aware of the universal drive for freedom; and Sekou's own restless struggle for liberation becomes understandable. He is a serious interpreter of history. It is instructional that the section in "Nativity," which details most of the resistance workers, including King and Rodney, begins by reaffirming self-sufficiency and self-actualization. History is that important in Sekou's aesthetics. For him it is particularly important in liberation, especially in warrior success against giants of "ill *norte*" in collusion with missionaries. This is suggested in "If 3 Escape" from *Images in the Yard*, which speaks of Zulus defeating British troops in spite of the sophisticated arms of the latter.

The Role of Education

Most revolutionaries recognize the power of education in initiating the youth into the new thinking and even in indoctrinating them. Sekou is too shrewd not to recognize the importance of the educational grounding if love's labors are not to be lost on the journey to liberation. Besides, he has a genuine interest in educating the children of St. Martin as a means of introducing them to their true culture, of which the curriculum should consists, and in passing on the wisdom of the aged. This latter is all the more important, he insists, in "Who Will Save the Children": "These times, where wisdom of age is outlawed."[39] He realizes also that children have some unlearning to do, steeped as they are in the colonial culture that undermines personal and national self-esteem. In his very first volume, he resolutely declares:

For our children will plant
. . . we must teach the children
Their children shall tend the crops
. . . they will be taught[40]

But education and relearning are not confined to the youth.

National Symbols of St. Martin is by definition a handbook, a tool of learning, and a national curricular resource. The dust jacket blurb is explicit on this: "*The National Symbols* does not shy away from a perceived social responsibility to be a valuable reference and a primary text for the nation's education and information systems." That it will serve the purpose of liberation is almost incidental. This illustrates St. Martin's indebtedness to the man and gives his mission an ethos of sincerity.

Sekou's interest in education is not merely motivated by his liberation program. He chafes over wasted potential and resultant loss to the individuals and lack in national resources. In early titles, the concerns are mundane but important: young children out too late, their poverty of spirit described as "mental exhaustion,"[41] and their innocent and simplistic treatment of the boy-girl relationship.[42]

The latest work devotes two poems to St. Martin's children. In descipling them, unity and patriotism are critical; they must "fight to be.long&love one another."[43] They are to avoid the imperial indoctrination of the "bastard motherlands" France and The Netherlands as well as the socialization of alienation that comes from the new greed of elites. "st. martin children II" is particularly moving as this committed patriot swears by his writing and his poem that his life and person are devoted to the children. It climaxes with these noble lines:

> this is your poem . . .
> it is a ponum of yes, my love
> i will never leave you.

The children symbolize St. Martin and its future. Sekou's poetry will itself help to mold Caribbean manhood, which "is not constructed in Caribbean schools."[44] These institutions need to be liberated from irrelevant and moribund curricula, he suggests.

"Look Them" and "Schools," both from *Images in the Yard*, have much to say about the socialization and education of youth, and the relevance to liberation is clear. In the former, the poet is anxious that the children are not re-enslaved through a culture of muzzling silence. In the latter, he questions the school program, which lacks genuine intellectualism to the extent that Einstein's theory is marginalized, and the spirit of wonder and curiosity is barely alive. This curriculum is not fit for a progressive generation. In *Born Here* Sekou would also like the creole tongue, the language with which so many of the people grapple with life, given some space in the school curriculum. Writing in 1986, this was a still fairly progressive view. Creole tongue is not just "badspeak," it is about creolizing culture and emphasizing the importance of what is indigenous. He accordingly calls the people

> To your schools / Seated on the crown
> Of this nation's tongue / Teaching in what we speak
> To break the leaching syndrome
> The insecurities and in-fluencies[45]

Sekou elevates *nation language*, or nation tongue as he terms it, by practice; and he does so here by precept. For him, children must be put in a learning environment where they can dream change, such as having St. Martin people own more of the means of production. Thus, the casino man's son in *Nativity* has Sekou's blessing. St. Martin ownership is central to Sekou's own vision, and the son is really a mouthpiece of the author. Another monologue, "Goin' School," emphasizes the importance of education in spite of discouraging employment prospects and an illogical emphasis on experience as a qualification. Education is still an open gate to success as the use of a gate as a prop intriguingly suggests. That success is important since youth has a proactive role in nation building. After all, "youth . . . got eyes. Like somebody wahn make us believe like our kind born to serve other people instead ah working together for we oanself." Education is critical for instilling these values.

Whether it is with children or adults, education is

a basis of liberation. Research into the past, including the African past, is a critical aspect of that education: "Research your history Africans / Like scholars / Not like the European liars"[46] is also applicable to the people of St. Martin. It will help to correct the miseducation that allows the nation's heroes to bleed to death,[47] and Sekou's pages are filled with heroes as we have seen. Such learning will help the people to respect and make friends with Self and bolster patriotism. "Plastic High" highlights those who lack self-esteem, which is why they straighten their hair and have no stomach for the fight for their mother-nation.[48] Learning and research are particularly applicable to the children in whose curriculum science and subjects of developmental value should feature. He ends the poem "Quimbé" in *Quimbé* with this clarion call: "GIVE US OUR CHILDREN / give us science give us business." Education for independence has to be comprehensive; it is not just politics and poetry.

The Purpose of Liberation

Inevitably, we have already adumbrated the purposes of liberation, but it seems necessary to more sharply focus on them in a final brief section of this chapter. For a general statement of Sekou's purpose, one does not necessarily have to interpret the poems. In 1999, he states it explicitly in the essay, "Colony, Territory or Partner?"

> Given the state of our mothernation, could there be a singular issue more important than to pledge one's humble self to work, study, build for and prosper from the political independence, cultural dynamism, social and economic development, and eventual unification of Sweet St. Martin Land?[49]

Two words, "independence" and "unification" say it all, or nearly. However, these words are means to an end. Some 15 years before, the poet-warrior concretizes his purpose in respects of benefits to the people by endorsing Bishop's revolutionary agenda in Grenada:

> ... this revolution is for work, food, for decent housing and health services, and for a bright future for our children and great grand children. The benefits of the revolution will be given to everyone ... Let us all unite as one.[50]

Based on the Bishop text, a decent standard of living with everyone enjoying the basic necessities of life is a goal. However, this requires preliminary changes and developments. We must, for a start "cast off the chains / That bound our entity / In the holds of poverty" where "chains" and "holds" suggest neoslavery.[51] He realizes that freedom has to be fought because rulers do not surrender power tamely. It has to be wrested

From the chalice of destiny
And forged upon the anvil
Of our Self-Determination[52]

The imagery here suggests great energy and exertion. No feeble investment can achieve liberation and self-determination.

Territorial ownership of St. Martin by the people (and even spiritual ownership) is a key goal for Sekou and the word "own" or "oan" is a constant in his work. The poem "This is our Land" in *Maroon Lives*, with its Calibanic resonance, ostensibly about South Africa can just as easily apply to St. Martin. And how much more emphatically, even if unconventionally, can total ownership and claim be stated than to say the mission in South Africa transcends civil rights or just "Sharing a bench / or shit-house with whites." Justice, equality, and rights do have their place as Camille says in "The Wake," but for Sekou these are subsumed under liberation and total possession.

The author pays attention to details such as, the evils that must be eliminated from among the people. He mentions a few in "Doped Up Roughings" including drugs, theft, and child abuse. The strident imagery conveys something of his attitude to these evils among the young:

I am this schoolgirl in your daughter's class--
    let hard-back man piss on me
                          on great bay beach
    becausin' I'm cracking up for this white stuff[53]

The economy of language here and power of suggestion are simply enthralling.

One of Sekou's aim is to liberate St. Martin from paralyzing and backward-looking ideologies. In eliminating St. Martin from hunger, he would dull the desire for a distant Eden, a pie in the sky. "I am in search of pure images of hunger and happiness," he says in "Manna From Heaven" and

Blessed be
The struggle of the Black Man
For it will be
The salvation of the world
The liberation of man and woman

. . .
Work the land

. . .
No manna will fall from heaven[54]

In "Love Song" from the same volume, *For the Mighty Gods* he cynically pronounces

Let the Great Gods keep salvation in heaven
On earth I desire only You![55]

This is addressed to a lover, but St. Martin is also his love. Paradise on earth requires work, and Sekou wishes to liberate his people to work for themselves and struggle for their independence.

Finally, he wants the people of St. Martin to invest in the future of their country, whether it is in the land, on the sea, or taking to the streets in agitation. Hopefully, his own work will prepare the people to labor towards birthing the new dawn. Given his favorite imagery of seeds, birthing is an appropriate purpose. In these lines from *Born Here*, he uses that imagery purposefully and to great effect:

Put your hands
Between the legs of this island
And bury seminal seeds
For bountiful tomorrows.[56]

4

SEKOU AND CULTURE

Defining Culture

Culture is an amorphous concept, which is not very easily defined to everyone's satisfaction. UNESCO defines it in this way:

> Culture is the whole complex of distinctive spiritual, material, intellectual and emotional features that characterize a society or social group. It includes not only arts and letters, but also modes of life, the fundamental rights of the human being, value systems, traditions and beliefs.[1]

When Peter Minshall observes that "the poem, the song, the painting is but water drawn from the well of the people,"[2] he is describing culture in poetic language. Rex Nettleford includes goods and products as manifestations of culture even though he highlights customs, religions, rituals, songs, stories, dances, and spirit.[3]

From these explanations it is evident that culture is not just ackee and saltfish in Jamaica, calypso and pan in Trinidad and Tobago, Kadooment in Barbados, Kwéyòl and Carib art in Dominica, or guavaberry in St. Martin. Not many of Sekou's reviewers have examined his concept of and focus on culture.

In fact, he has demonstrated a firm grasp of the comprehensiveness of the concept and its role in national development. This chapter purports to address this aspect of his work.

Sekou's epic poem "Nativity" is really a poetic thesis on culture, and one suspects it is a unique piece. In her introduction to *Nativity*, Gumbs understands:

> *Nativity* is a living culture of our collective labor, love, and rites of liberation. Caribbean poetry, the soul and "culture manifest" of Caribbean dance, speech, song, and literature, is enriched herein by Lasana M. Sekou's unique style and tough craftsmanship.

This summary clarifies that although Sekou gives much attention to culture as the arts to a great extent, as is the conventional tendency, he treats it as a much more fundamental phenomenon, which critically connects with his central theme of nation building and liberation.

Generally regarded as a major work, *The Salt Reaper* is about culture albeit less overtly than *Nativity*. Ervin Beck is relevant when commenting on the former; he pronounces that "the theme of these poems is culture and nation building more so than revolution."[4] The centrality of culture to Sekou's understanding of life, development, and social progress can be illustrated from his essays as well as the fiction. In her introduction to *Love Songs Make You Cry*,

Jeffry, who always connects Sekou with culture, had this to say about the stories. "The glimpses into the daily lives of the people living on the island, past and present, help to immortalize the customs and traditions of the cultural dimension of these stories."[5] This is exactly what culture is about, and, consciously or not, Sekou is constantly trafficking in culture, whether in St. Martin, the Caribbean, the Americas or Africa, or a combination. And you cannot shut Sekou out, however you widen the concept. In a celebratory speech, the same Jeffry has called culture as seen in *Nativity* "a song of bravery, courage, struggle and trials." In his roll call of heroes of various passions, ideologies, and toils, who has illustrated this more amply than Sekou?

Culture and Economy

Some development economists tend to treat the arts, which are a dimension of culture, as mere entertainment and as dichotomous to economy, which is about the means and factors of development, crudely put. Indeed, rightly construed, culture is the true matrix of development. Those of us with an interest in culture are pleased that renowned regional economist (we do not necessarily endorse all of his views), Arthur Lewis, had a similar view of cultural products.

It is his position that: "A society without the creative arts is a cultural desert . . . Music, literature, and art are as important a part of the heritage of mankind as are science and morals."[6]

Sekou ties culture closely to economy. "Culture is work" is the emphatic line which opens "Nativity." Although he may here be suggesting that armchair revolutionaries are irrelevant, it is evident that tilling of the soil "for grounds to give up fruits and / so soil turned over to beauty black / rich and fertile" is culture. Although it is true that "bitter work brought us here," there will be beauty and art in cultivation in the new dispensation. This is especially so as we possess the green fields in which we toil and not depend on degrading concessions and be backyard basins. In that way we will not "catch aids of multinastiness / penetration from strange / invading business."[7] The sexual imagery does not obscure the fact that he could be dealing with economic policy generated by the US Caribbean Basin Initiative.

Throughout "Nativity" imagery and language of productivity indicate that for Sekou culture is no flabby underbelly. It is about "a St. Lucia mosera of markets and painting to produce / scattering breadfruits." It is undoing the parasitic work of conquistadors, and building "living monuments from aloe / & maize & calabash & gold & mold & correct /

our New World self." Significantly, the poem ends on work as it began: "For so long have the People worked / And endless songs done sung / And still so many accounts to give Life." Sekou's concept of culture is a wholesome and holistic one.

As a "custom of the people," work is culture. The beauty of such work is celebrated in "Up from the Land" in *Mothernation*:

> it is a beauty
> to see the people work
> cultivating the land
> and making preparations for life

In this poem, again there seems to be an indissoluble tie between livelihood and art. The lyric beauty of these lines almost robs toil of its arduousness though we know the reality is different from the romantic aura:

> The ground farmer
> sings an opulent Black song of golden soil
> dance steps to seed the land
> beat green drums of sustenance
> to weave cool running hands of water

Although "My Land" in *The Salt Reaper* is about his patria, it is shot through with imagery from cultivation in words like "ripeness," "manna," "pen," "flocks," "ram" and "lamb" along with the "e-language" of "template," "frame," and "modem."

There is certainly no doubt in Sekou's mind that political independence is a means to an end, which is social and material development; and discipline and production are on the road map to nation building. This is evident in *Big Up St. Martin*.[8] And in "For Exiles" from *Maroon Lives* he states in emphatic monosyllabic words, for the most part: "We must free and feed ourselves." The juxtaposition of free and feed and the alliteration withal must not be missed. He repeats the same sentiment in *Born Here*: "Isn't it true that freedom means feeding ourselves?"[9]

The physical environment of a country which shapes and is shaped by the people in a dialectical relationship is culture, and the environment is part of the country's economic asset. It is not surprising that Beck sees *The Salt Reaper*, which centers on salt ponds and salt workers, as dealing with culture. And as Liverpool observes, "Sekou is the salt reaper, for his land, his labors, his ideals, and his values have been, to a large extent, fashioned by the salt ponds, St. Martin's historical 'plantation'." Slave and predatory labor in the ponds "through the briny ages" were the backbone of the economy—an economy that was beggarly for the masses. The bread it brought was "bitter lice bite crumbs for you."[10]

It was nevertheless the landscape, not only the salt, but shrimp and fish for food and trade that ensured the survival of the people. And yet the pond must be preserved and honored as part of the natural heritage and as a monument to ancestral labor rather than be allowed to degenerate into the "nation's stench" in an act of retaliation. In some form or fashion, the pond will ever be there as part of the landscape even as an inspirer of poems, not of love but of righteous anger from the likes of Sekou, the conscience of the nation. Rather they will be "pond salt rhymes."

It is worth observing here that culture is not necessarily always an approval word. Culture is dynamic, and Sekou recognizes that aspects of culture need to be changed so "culture is borning change." And as he holds the current state of the salt pond up to public view, he hopes for change in keeping with his view of the emerging society.

Attention is also given to the bays like Great Bay, which are part of the environment, and which are haunts of the tourist industry. Issues of use and ownership arise, and the persona in the monologue "Look Trouble" was skeptical of plans for developing Marigot, which included more hotels and "trade port." In Sekou's view, "the little S'Maatiner 'ain no way in those plans." The message is that the cultural environment needs to be available for the enjoyment of the people. They must be free to enjoy the "ponds, lagoon, and flatlands."[11] It is interesting how in "Saline" from *Quimbé* the bays and the salt come together in a poem of dance, celebrating, as it were, the seamlessness of the culture when it operates as it should: "and show me how we use to lift our feet / in and out the saltpans of great bay and grand case." For the poet, Great Bay Beach must at least be safe for school girls, at the very least.

Folk Culture

Whether in the form of proverbial wisdom as detailed in *National Symbols of St. Martin*, native foods, creole remedies, art, customs and religion, or history, folklores are powerful manifestations and definers of the national culture. This is because they have antedated the penetration and iconoclastic intervention of Europeans and survived, albeit not intact, because of their elemental force.

The extensive treatment Sekou gives to folklore stems from his abiding patriotism and rootedness; he is fully aware of their potential to underpin revolution and nation building, given their provenance. Culture, then, is integral to his overarching purpose. "Nativity" is the obvious mine for folk culture, but Sekou scatters references to folklore throughout his work to add charm and spice and to illuminate. Folk material also aids accessibility to his poems, which have a public function. Gumbs rightly points out that "Nativity" is "studded with the people's daily living and produce." This idea connects neatly with our previous section because folk is about economic matters also.

St. Martin foods speak to initiative and industry as well as self-reliance and are particularly important in Caribbean countries with oversized import food bills and the consequent drain on foreign exchange. So the foods are there, some common to the Caribbean, some associated with Taino Indian ancestors, some are products of the specific island environment, and some terms like "nyam" are of African origin. They include dumpling, cassava meal, arrowroot, callaloo and okra soup, goat water, black-eyed peas, sorrel and soursop, guavaberry of course, and "chicken leg and rum, drunk at election time like slave X-mas." So he loses no chance to be cynical about election styles while rejecting an aspect of the culture. The food sector of culture speaks to the need for indigenization; it is getting on

with this conch & dumpling business
and
if
it
passionfruit
you
seek:

> boil together mauby bark
> anise seeds
> nutmeg(from Grenada)skin.[12]

Here again foods become the fabric of the poem while inspiring it.

An example of a hearty meal referred to as a knight's breakfast table is given in the story, "Brotherhood of the Spurs." It reflects a kind of Caribbean unity in the selection of foods from around the region. The meal consists of

> salt fish, with thin, soft cucumber slices and diced onions, johnnycakes, hot bakes with butter dripping warm . . . jelly for bread, mackerel, steaming bush teas stirred with brown sugar from St. Kitts, cocoa tea from Dominica, coffee . . . from Hope Estate grounded in Grand Case, creamy porridges made . . . with milk from Gaspard Baly and Flemming's fat-titty cattle. Cinnamon and nutmeg from Grenada were stuck in or grated over corn or arrowroot pap.[13]

A breakfast indeed fit for a king or a true St. Martin peasant. The emphasis on island produce is significant, and with Caribbean Community and Common Market going before it comes, it would seem Sekou suggests that Caribbean unity should begin at the level of the people and their culture rather than the leaders and politics.

Diversity in the use of native foods demonstrating

economy was also of interest. Great Grandmother "T" of the monologues tells us that they did not only make porridge from the arrow-root tuber. It was used in laundry. "Vie used to make porridge with it, and starch vie clothes"; and we get a glimpse into creole technology. "The mens would poun' the arrow-root and vie would ring it so."[14]

Caribbean remedies are closely connected with the foods, and some remedies are foods. Herbal remedies have acquired status today with the endorsement of the likes of Britain's Prince Charles. In Sekou they need no such prestigious external legitimization, trusting as he does the ancestral wisdom, which "researched" and produced them. Some drinks such as mauby, anise seeds, nutmeg skin, and lime juice have general invigorating and refreshing value. Breadfruit leaves drink, however, has curative properties for the popular, debilitating disease, diabetes, which is a major killer. Some of us may have to drink in faith, but "give us science" too, Sekou demands in *Quimbé*, in order to enhance and create new medicines from those based on the wisdom of the ancients. The succeeding lines reveal some of the therapeutic processes inherent in our herbs:

and from gardens pick new medicines
healings squeezed from our leaves &

herbs & bushes of health & Seacolean
nursing
/tizanne.bushteas.calm nerves.purge.
sea bath.bush baths.all blue & green
water cleansing us from coard envy
freshen us up to solidarity <>[15]

There is so much in these lines. Sekou presents no
tension between the herbal cures and conventional
medicine judged by the way the famous nurse, Mary
Seacole, is woven into the lines. The calming and
purging properties bring not just physical but emotional healing to the extent of eliminating envy and
clearing minds to think thoughts of solidarity. National cohesion and nation building are never far
from the poet's consciousness.

Customs and religion are also components of the
culture, and Sekou focuses on some that are regional. For example, Ademus' wife in "The Wake" saved
money by sous-sous, a well known Yoruba saving system. In death, the same Ademus appeared to have
needed a drink, from the behavior of a drunken guest
who "staggered over and peed the rum out." The company catered to Ademus' thirst by dropping a few sips
of Miss Ruby's fine guavaberry in the center of the
grounding. Drops of liquor are used on other occa-
sions in the region to secure fellowship of the dead.
What in some places is referred to as "taking leave of

the dead" was practiced in the same story when Ademus' granddaughter placed her cheek against his. Not to be missed is the fact that the person responsible for finally closing the coffin was "the old woman of herbal and Ponum secrets."

No culture is really superior to another, and in Sekou's universe mainstream (whatever these are) and folk religions have parallel if not equal value. Reference was made in chapter 3 to the common pantheon in which Sekou has placed Zeus, Krishna, and Christ. In "Nativity" he includes Muhammad, African Legba, Jamaican Kumina, and others, all on the same level. In this way, he is inclusive of all the ethnic groups in the region, while preserving a distinctive African bias. Of course, Rastafarianism has a place and their Selassie, like Kumina, is an African retention in Caribbean culture. Still forbidden on some Caribbean statute books, religions like Voodoo and Santeria and folk beliefs like obeah are not given any pejorative treatment by Sekou. In *Moods for Isis* he summons ancestral spirits positively:

Fill the night air
With magic calls
of Shango rituals
revoke . . . revoke
The voodoo rites for freedom and food
for work and strength.[16]

"See the Idren," one of the longest poems in *Born Here*, is obviously about the Rastafarian brethren. Their doctrine and music are highlighted, and the charge on Babylon recurs like a restless chorus. In addition to the threat to unfavorable political directorates symbolized by Babylon, there is direct opposition to the church, especially the "Roman" Church. In the poem the "bretheren" await the trumpet from another prophet: "A Dread sound / To tremble the seat of Babylon / To topple the crown of Rome." There is suggestion here of Haile Selassie I as an alternate prophet. This is emphasized in an implicit challenge to Jesus Christ, the biblical headstone of the corner: "When we, the Stone the builder refused / Shall be the head-corner stone." Sekou is in the Rastafarian corner, big time.

One is not surprised at Sekou's accommodation of Rastafarian, for they offer an alternative explanation (whether we are skeptical or not) of the human and Caribbean realities and an alternative to Eurocentrism. Open and liberal as he is, he would wish to extract from Rasta positive values and vibes for his own "commonwealth." He is not unhappy about their "prophetizing the fall of the wicked regime,"[17] because in some respects he has a common cause, and it is to their credit that they are creative in ideology and the arts. He therefore frowns on those who release from prison "punked-out rolling stones / But cut Rasta locks."[18] The activities or inactivities of the Christian churches in the face of human ills come off poorly in comparison to Rasta deeds. So he questions about a pregnant "illegal" immigrant:

And where are the churches now
The righteous servants of God and Man
While this Caribbean Mary / Went without shelter[19]

Again, he turns Christianity on its head with these biblical references; the imagery such as "fork-tongues" and "raycons" are, to say the least, neither kind nor polite. Indeed, as culture man he (I suppose) "prophetizes" the locking up of churches. At least they are already closed to the oppressed. In the introduction to *For the Mighty Gods*, Amiri Baraka, who finds several varieties of narcotics more satisfying than God, has this evaluation of Sekou's reaction to deity:

But I think for all the swarm of metaphysical reference that does attach itself to this young poet's work from time to time, after the image-content mode of Black cultural nationalism, Lasana's use of the Gods is positive.

Maybe; but he is more positive about gods of African provenance than of European, and I have little doubt the former would occupy the superior places in any hierarchy of his pantheon.

Festivals and rituals, usually of folk origin, do not escape Sekou's wide-angled cultural lens. Carnival is mentioned associated especially with Trinidad as well as its practice in various forms elsewhere. Minshall, an exponent of the big carnival band is honored in "Nativity." Also mentioned is crop-over in Barbados, which not only celebrates the end of crop and its feverish activities but once provided the enslaved with the opportunity to burn in revenge Mr. Harding who represents the merciless masters. Nana Mandisa's ritual "washing" of a young lady before her journey to the cruel west in *Brotherhood of the Spurs* is interesting, and similarities have persisted in some Caribbean countries.[20]

Culture and the Arts

Among the arts, Sekou concentrates on music and poetry. (Some of the music is folk, but it is convenient to deal with all music in this section.) Sekou knows his Caribbean music, and he carefully chooses to emphasize those works and artists that underpin revolution and nation building. He leaves one in no doubt as to who his icons are. With his signature instrument of the region, pan is celebrated. Arguably, it is the only percussion instrument invented in the twentieth century, and it is in a sense a symbol of the pan-Caribbean world. He captures both this idea and the ringing rhythm of pan in these "Nativity" lines:

> if you think you loss the pangs
> and panalanglangsteelarkestras
> arkestrating pan vibes
> > pan Caribbean
> > pan *Caribe*
> > pan *Antilles*
> > pan people are nation (pan)
> > the world pan
> > against apartheid
> > and panapanfree
> pan you, pan eye, pan *oui*

The political overtones are evident. As Liverpool observes, the passing on to the young of a country's folklore and symbols is never neutral.[21] This is true of oppressors, and it is also true of would-be liberators such as Sekou.

Pan's twin calypso or kaiso, also Caribbeanized with its penchant for making trenchant social comments and critiques, grabs Sekou's attention. He is in a sense a poet-calypsonian, and this thinking is aided by the performance rhythms crafted into his lines. Calypsonians are makers and mediators of culture, and Sekou salutes them old and new: Kitchener, Black Stalin, Sparrow, Rose, and in a very early poem the Mighty Duke, to whom he imputes an instructional function which focuses on negritude: "We must teach the children / black is back."[22]

Sekou finds reggae, a music of protest, obviously attractive. The association with Bob Marley, a Jamaican national hero and a Sekou and international icon, adds importance to the music. Marley earns his own poem in *Born Here*, where he is hailed as poet, prophet, high priest, and shaman, making it clear that he is revered both for his art and his philosophy. If Marley is a prophet, Sekou is his apostle. Marley is one of his six great Ms, his messiahs: Marcus Garvey, Martin Luther King, Jr., Malcolm X, Maurice Bishop, and Nelson Mandela being the others.

Other popular musicians like the Wailers and the Burning Flames and African music directly represented "in de drum" are highlighted. Drum music is particularly important in masquerade dancing and j'ouvert jamming related to carnival. It suits Sekou to integrate these arts of pan and drum of Caribbean and Africa and to capture their effect in his lines:

Bragadangbam! boom si kai si ka boom di
la la la la la day
come like Man born to Pan
draped in moses
& fingerprints
of steel palms
& goatskins
of drums.[23]

In his voracious reading, Sekou encountered several poets writing in English (including some of those translated into English from the Spanish-, Papiamentu-, French- and Dutch-speaking Caribbean region and Latin America). Those he cites in "Nativity" share some affinity with his militant work—his tone of protest or the revolutionary agenda. Commentators have drawn comparison between the structure of Kamau Brathwaite's *Arrivants* and "Nativity."[24] Dr. Maria van Enckevort, for instance, has commented on the influence of what she calls Brathwaite's "video style" on Sekou.[25] She is referring to those unique verbal artifices which he frequently employs. Brathwaite gets much space with his "singing arrivants" for example or in these "Nativity" lines: "Kamau-an-found beats in warrior silence / mek night march through cosmic cadenza." Brathwaite's structural inventions and his unconventional diction by themselves make him a poet of protest, in spirit at least. This alone guarantees a Sekou-Kamau nexus in radical writing, apart from the fact that Brathwaite is a recognized poet of resistance.

Next to Brathwaite is Michael Smith, a Rastafarian revolutionary in his own way with the exaltation of Jah music in his dub poetry associated with a futuristic if not an apocalyptic vision:

and we / like burning flame fueling Zion Train
coming-it-a-come / coming-it-a-come . . .

comingitacome / coming it a come ...
through a true middle passage infested[26]

Writing out of London, but of Jamaican origin, Linton Kwesi Johnson is a leading nation language and performance poet. Sekou, therefore, has much in common with him. Poet of the 1981 Brixton ghetto riots, his "dread beat an' blood" poems performed to music celebrate and promote black resistance to those London racist attacks. "Dem say: di babylan dem went too far." This cements the affinity with Sekou for whom resistance inheres in Caribbean culture. Encouraged very likely by Kwesi's work, he visited Brixton in person and in poetry "not so much for the dead and gone / but for sights of the alive and coming"[27] and because of the poet's interest in the black diaspora. The poem, "While in London" ends with this revealing line: "*you can't paint over anger.*" Fortunately for Sekou, he can channel it through his art. Paul Keens-Douglas of "Tante Merle" and "cunny jamma oman" of Louise Bennett of Jamaica are in some ways kindred spirits with Johnson and Sekou in the primacy they give to creole language and in their role as griots; so they too are celebrated.

In the Caribbean cultural continuum, other creative and philosophical writings feature. Essentially classical, Derek Walcott is not above using nation language:

Man I suck me tooth when I hear
How dem croptime fiddlers lie
And de wailing, kiss-me-arse flutes
That bring water to me eye![28]

He expresses some angst, though, over choosing "Between this Africa and the English tongue I love." For Sekou no such choice is necessary as each has its place even if Africa and St. Martin loom larger than Europe in his writings. Like Sekou, Lamming is a decolonizer as his landmark novel *In the Castle of My Skin* and other writings show, and with Brathwaite he has supported local and regional publishing and consequently national and Caribbean development by choosing to publish in House of Nehesi Publishers. This fuels the shift from a psychology of dependence to a culture of self-reliance, a culture of

    I&I Self

        determine

            nation[29]

Sekou gives an honored place in Caribbean literary culture to Trinidadian-born leftist philosopher, C.L.R. James whose *The Black Jacobins* explains Toussaint, that black liberating hero of the Haitian revolution. Like Sekou, he exposed racism and became an advocate of Caribbean independence. In his other major work, *Beyond the Boundary*, he saw cricket as art and its emphasis on fair play as ethics. Indeed, cricket was used as an ethical metaphor of the colonizer. Sekou himself understood it seems the meaning of cricket beyond the boundary in his carping criticism of the West Indians who played the *game* in apartheid South Africa. Lamming himself had his own encounter with James, which was not necessarily always positive.[30]

This study does not cover Sekou's survey of creative writers who contribute ideas to liberation, decolonization, and nation building, but those we allude to are significant and representative. Sekou has never doubted the role of art in the march toward independence. He has clearly delineated the place of art and the role of artists in the independence train. With others like Samuel Selvon and Guillén, these illustrate that cultural elements island hop, transcending even language barriers. To prove this, he sprinkles Spanish, Kwéyòl, Papiamentu, French, and Dutch in his work, as befitting his island, with its present-day French and Netherlands overlordship. Pico Iver in an issue of *Time* magazine commenting on Walcott's *Hymns for the Indigo Hour* observed: "If the multiculturalists who govern the academy were worthy of a gospel, they would need to look no further." It should not be thought robbery if I suggest that Sekou's work deserves a shelf nearby.

It is important to point out that Sekou does not doubt the power of his poetry to shape consciousness and culture. He is one of the "P.O.W. (Poets of War)":

I am here . . . a poet of war
For I called upon the name of peace, progress and Allah
       and in my search for Truth
       I bruised against their evil and injustice
. . . . . . this is my crime[31]

As early then as *Moods for Isis* he was announcing that his poetry was not neutral. The perceptive Badejo has commented on this urge to communicate through Sekou's art.[32] Making a similar claim, Wycliffe Smith focuses the poetic message more sharply on children, citing these lines from "Homeland Harvest":

I have sown here songs for you
While you slept on frigid limbo's bed
I bring this homeland harvest
Grown from your long planting
To feed our children[33]

Poetry is one of Sekou's vehicles for passing on heritage and legacy of value. And there is something genuinely moving in the way Sekou contemplates the absence of the poet from the culture, in the "doxology" of *Moods for Isis*:

And when

There are no more poets
Who will weep for Mother Earth
. . .
And when
There are no more poets
Who will know of life

And, one might add, "who will sing a song for the children?"

Culture and History

History is the foundation of culture, and Lasana M. Sekou is obviously an encyclopedic reader of Caribbean history and the history of those countries that have impacted both positively and negatively thereon. Sekou's wide swathe of historical knowledge takes in countries as small as Montserrat, with its 1768 slave uprising, or as large as Africa, motherland of many. Chronologically, he recognizes those who came before Columbus and those who came after bringing their colonial and indentured freight. In this way, he can identify various and varied currents that flow into a sea of Caribbean culture, which is necessarily an amalgam. He is also in a position to harvest heroes and templates worldwide, especially those with liberation values and records such as the African general Hannibal who crossed the Alps in 218 B.C. and routed the Roman armies. In building a culture of achievement, African, Caribbean and pan-American heroes are critical.

In recognizing the place of pre-Columbian peoples like Ciboneys and Tainos, he considers also the Olmecs, Mayans, and Aztecs. These are important in a culture of self-respect because cities like Paris and London would have been shanty towns in comparison when these civilizations were at their zenith.

In the context of culture, Sekou reminds us that Africa is more than a source of slaves, in this couplet:

From Africa comes only gods
        said the Greeks
Out of Africa comes always something new
        said the Arabs.[34]

5

THE SEKOU AESTHETICS

A "Sekou School"

When Badejo writes of "the Sekou school," he means more than his resistance poetry and the polemical content of his work. He includes his "powerful, guided, verbal missiles against every target of colonialism and divisiveness . . . His voice rises above the mundane, far above the pedantic, and curls up like a smoke signal to all the sleeping warriors of the nation."[1] Reviewing *Nativity* in 1988, I noted that "the poet aims missiles of virile words, but he breaks down to build 'upful / & right / glistening cities / and own green fields' conveying a sense of strength, freshness, spontaneity and Caribbean authenticity."[2]

There is an identifiable school of resistance poetry in which the Guyanese poet Martin Carter; Césaire; and Brathwaite, arguably a Sekou mentor, belong. Although not designating it a school, Allen-Agostini recognizes the genre in her review of *The Salt Reaper* and *37 Poems*. And Carter himself has labeled a collection of his poems as *Poems of Resistance*, and these led to his imprisonment. It is a matter for speculation what Sekou's fate would have been if he had lived in a Guyana. Yet in a curious way his resistance writings may have helped preserve a modicum of democracy in St. Martin even if it is the "democrazy" brand.

There is a Sekou school in the sense that he is an exemplar both in his revolutionary ways and in his unique style and idiom. Writing out of St. Martin, the work of Drisana Deborah Jack and Esther Gumbs resonate Sekou. One echoes Sekou the revolutionary and rebel and the other, as I have written elsewhere, resembles him as an impassioned advocate of traditional values and folkways.[3] It is probably easy to find creative writers who engage in elements of Sekou's style and crafting whether it is nation language, orality, imagery, irony and satire, functional misspelling, fractured words, shocking metaphors, and plain but powerful statements and more. Sekou, however, stands alone in their combination and the depth and breadth to which he explores and exploits them within the bounds of art. This, in part, is the Sekou school.

The Sekou school is essentially Caribbean with an African flavor. In *Born Here*, he begins the poem "On Caribbean Aesthetics" with these fascinating lines:

I have watched my fathers
Dancing in the shadow of iguanas
Skanking in the light of goatskin drums
In the arch of Legba's limbo

The yoking of Legba the linguist with limbo underscores the Caribbean-African basis of the aesthetic. The poem is both a statement and a demonstration of his poetics. His poems embody ancestral images and rhythms, the sound of "Shango's hammer"; his theme is Caribbean people "stooped in labor." Centipedes, mangoes, and guava stir him more than wintry daffodils. His tongue is flexible, free to curse if he wishes in calypso style with Caliban as a prototype. Poetry is ultimately a journey into self-discovery. "It is time for them our Family / To find the Eden Place of Peace." I see some parallel with J.C. Aboud, who wrote:

I cannot arrange my words vertically
And make announcements of victory.
My lines must contain the zip of Tradewinds
And the pattern of water splashed on sand.[4]

He indicates the rooting of his lines in the Caribbean experience and natural environment. The Jamaican sculptor Edna Manley wrote of a Jamaican boy who never left the heat of the St. Andrew plains but wrote of "the icy winds that pierce my Soul." However, imaginative this is, this kind of writing would be alien to the Sekou school and Aboud's thinking. When he uses images of snow, he usually is characterizing persons, philosophies, and products from unfriendly climes.

Sekou's "Nation Tongue"

Nation Language, a term popularized by Brathwaite, is variously referred to as dialect, creole, patois, and vernacular, even though there may be nuanced differences among some of these terms. One is referring to the language of folk, the language by which they understand and grapple with life, a language of realism. Sekou uses the people's idiom, and the rhythm of many poems is the music of their lives, sometimes harsh, sometimes tuneful. With this medium he "captures not just the palpable plight of the present but subliminal yearnings of the people and their subconscious quest for freedom."[5] One could have appropriately dealt with nation language, what Sekou himself calls "nation tongue," under the heading of folk culture, but does so here for convenience and because it is so liberally used by Sekou.

In promoting patriotism, self-respect, and interest in what is "of the people," nation language serves Sekou's purpose well. So the St. Martin lingo and the nation tongue of other Caribbean countries and territories run throughout "Nativity," the epic of culture, and other poems. Here is a typical quotation drawn from women's fashion:

> & wink away kan-kan jealous
> of
> our

women
backside
grace
likefollowfashionmonkey
in monkey shell crack to no sound.

These lines from *Mothernation* capture indigenous pronunciation:

and ven boats didn't tek back tobacco
dey tek cotton and sugar
dey tek salt
den dey tek us, salt of the earth again[6]

where the insistence on "dey tek" conveys the plundering of the land and the people and the predatory nature of colonialism which "tek" many of us in the Antilles for a ride. The up-to-date *37 Poems* with its polished journalistic tone does not eschew the people's language. The book generally features China, but the St. Martin poems in the collection reflect island rhythms and realities; so do not be surprised by a line like this: "buh wa t'is yu list'ning for?"[7] and the word "causin" meaning "because" crops up, too.

What is delightfully surprising is the way in which Sekou demonstrates intimate knowledge of the vernacular which is rooted in other Caribbean cultures. The following lines from "Nativity" refer to Dominica and it is interesting how he has written into this performance piece the Dominican pronunciation of river, and hill, for instance:

> Dominicawomanwidsweettongue balancing
> Bananalabor pon she head
> Pass by de reevah . . . forthnighting
> down de heel to load the boat by the sea.[8]

He weaves in so much of the local culture: the role of the river in the lives of folk and laborious toil and night work in the banana industry. Sekou's use of nation language is not patronizing, it is illuminating. The "cunny jamma oman scratch dungle heap for phoenix to come out" works similarly, but "fe phoenix" would have been even more authentic. And the words "bazoodi" from Trinidad and "antiman" as an epithet from the Caribbean become native to his lines with ease. Similarly, two words in "Nativity" like "fart" and "fascists" become readily imbedded in the same line: "& blow *boeren* fascists to fart's end." Eighteen years ago, I commented on the ease with which Sekou moves from formal to informal English and the analysis is still valid:

> The ease with which the poet steps from formal language to informal, from classical to creole, from elegiac to folk reflects an erudition a breadth of vision, and withal a 'grounding with his brothers' . . . in the Caribbean and its circumambient world.[9]

He mounts up with wings like eagle intellectually but also walks (with the people) and is not faint, and this is the more challenging. As he quarries words from the mines of recent reality to build new notions such as "digicam" and "bin Laden" (been laden), he still remains grounded to I & I phrases.

The fictions, alive with people from ordinary but real life, naturally lend themselves to nation tongue, given what we know of Sekou's ideology. In the monologues, Great Grandmother "T," who personifies the wisdom of a passing generation, without a high standard of formal learning, speaks in the *S'maatin* vernacular as might be expected. She is too important an oral source of history to discriminate against her parlance which, in any case, has its own validity: "All you know vie had a song for when slavery done? People still sing it when I was small: 'O po, slave . . .'" There is something of a contrast in "The Bad That Man and Woman Do." Addressing the issue of values and a protocol for women in dealing with others and with men, a young woman attempts to speak formally but lapses into dialect, which obviously comes more easily. The mix is common in certain walks of society: "And the mens dem laugh at us, some to our face . . . ."

In "The Snoring" and "Fatty and the Big House" from *Love Songs Make You Cry*, by using the community nicknames of characters like Fatty, Taata, Gas, and Weeze, Sekou gives another perspective to the idiom of the people. This is all consonant with an environment in which a Rasta brings bush tea to a sick pregnant girl and Miss Ohna selling mauby from a mayonnaise bottle. Very flexible on the tongue of the people, nation language can be ideal for spitting insult. In "The Snoring," a grandmother dismisses a teenager with these words: "Yu' put yo' foot back in here yo' pissytail nastiness an' I will kill you." Middle-class pretentiousness in the person of Wilfred is decried in the phrase: "full of shit about his public image." The formal language equivalent is never quite the same for cutting down someone with dispatch. Our example from "The Wake" in *Brotherhood of the Spurs* comes from Cyus who articulates his philosophy about love in the dialect he knows: "Gentlemen, they say when a man lowe too much it is that woman who goin' betray him. Oi doan know if it is so 'causin Oi lowe a whole lot, but that woman of moin is an angel."

In addition to what is now conventional nation language, Sekou creates his own by bending language to his will and creatively distorts when standard forms and spellings do not serve his purpose. Smith agrees. "In order to get certain linguistic effects, he often ignores the rules of grammar, style and spelling."[10] In a rather erudite review of *The Salt Reaper*, Dr. van Enckevort takes this further and connects Sekou's devices with an African tradition of orality and word-sculptures; and she rightly suggests that this aspect of the poet's nation language has been influenced by Brathwaite known for his "video style" writing. She supports her claim with this quote from Brathwaite: "In the African tradition, they use sculpture. Really, what I'm trying to do is to create word-sculptures on the page, but word-song for the ear."[11] Khair has also drawn attention to what he calls Sekou's "chiro-graphic" experimentation[12] with the word which he uses to describe his excursion into the visual dimension of the language. Sekou is a revolutionary poet in more senses than one.

These stylistic devices began as early as *Mother-nation* and *Quimbé* in 1991. Introducing the book launch back then, I observed that he "distorts to suit his purpose." This is what he is doing in lines like:

theylettingincurasolenians & rubians & gwadlupians
& martniqians & mericans & france-man & eyetalians
& indians & Chinese & mafians to run with the show
and make it right fo' we[13]

Such lines convey the incessant tide of immigration, and I am sure that words like "rubians" and "gwadlu-pians" are not as innocent as they seem. *Quimbé* be-gan to reveal some sound and visual effects: "and meh boy, if ahl yo' doan wahn see s'maatin people / go loco loco / leave the border wey it beeeeeeeeeeeeeeee."[14]

In "r'ass remnants" in *The Salt Reaper*, he weaves a poem out of acronyms:

bdt
bot
bvi
bwi
. . .
dwi
fod
fwi
. . .
dom-tom.&all
like cowbrands
poking usssssssssssssssss. still.

The acronyms—identifying the remaining colonial territories in the Caribbean region—work visually, they goad (poke) us like asses while branding us with an external identity. These devices are abiding elements of the Sekou trademark (in the poem quoted above, notice he rejects other people's imposed trademarks) as "title X," in *37 Poems* illustrates. Khair's introduction describes this best:

It is an index of his range as a poet that he also brings into play devices from concrete poetry or visual poetry. The poetry is meant to be read on the page instead of being heard. In this slim volume, a good example is the second poem, "title X," where both the X of the title and the plus-marks (+) used in the lines target the "marked man" in space as well as language. This man marked by the telescopic rifle-sights (crosshair of the dominant neo-imperial discourse due to his "cross" hair tellingly comes to be *all who look alike / my brothers, again, the dark mane / locks at the cross hairs.*

In a subtle way "locks" suggests his Rastafarian brethren, who are of course, marked. Again, Van Enckevort is right: "This style doesn't necessarily make for 'easy' reading but it adds to the epithet of the poet's nation language. And it is language that gives us our identity." That is the point; it is nation language, the Sekou brand, and it is highly functional even if at times intellectually challenging and teasing.

Sekou's multilingual background further enriches his brand of nation language. His linguistic heritage is broadened to include Spanish, Papiamentu, and even "Yankee," as Joyce Peters-McKenzie observes.[15] Smith, too, alludes to the linguistic effects Sekou achieves by juxtaposing several languages or dialects including, of course, the word-sound spoken by the people of St. Martin. In addition to linguistic effects, I believe he is suggesting that languages should be no barrier to the unity of the region. This at least is implicit. It is no accident that "Cradle of the Nation" in *The Salt Reaper* speaks in diverse tongues, while extolling "one destiny still."

Other Literary Devices

Sekou is well known for his highly *alliterative* style. University of the West Indies lecturer Joseph Pereira thinks it is overly so in a review of *Born Here*. I have observed that the poem "Nativity," published two years after *Born Here*, is characteristically alliterative (and for the most part functionally so), which suggests some reservation. Generally, Sekou's alliterations reveal a craftsman at work rather than mere fascination with a verbal artifice except perhaps in his first book where you find a line like, "Mentally malnutritioned meals daily,"[16] which is a bit prosy. When in *Mothernation* he writes the line "coveting and conquering" he is describing progressive action—one thing leading to another. In *Quimbé's* "movements" Sekou writes as a performance poet, and part of the polemical-rhetorical element is built in, resulting in an alliteration of 't.'

> From tiananmen
> > to tbilisi
> > to trinidad
> > to township fever
> > . . .
> it is the same old thing[17]

One can imagine the voice rising with each line to a crescendo effect.

The poet does it even more intriguingly and to

richer emotional effect. In his "Nativity," he brings variation into the alliteration with a play on the words: "a- / cross to bear bare through barren wilds / of fields." "Bare" and "barren" emphasize each other and the landscape in which culture is to be planted securing a cumulative effect; or he may use the device to express contradictions and ironies as in "fêting you up / feeling you up."[18] And in a line already quoted in connection with diction, Sekou uses it to mock apartheid, for instance, and denunciate it by yoking "fascist" and "fart's." In folk culture, there is something highly derogatory in the juxtaposition of "fascists" and "fart." He uses it in an even more mature fashion in contrasts such as "missionary" and "mercenary" and "liberal liars" making stark the incongruity. In the vein of maturity, he perhaps uses alliteration less in the latest works, but it serves his purpose for liquid lyric movement as in "to love thy cultures, seedings to the joyous conception / motherings for another forever of futures / become the strength bristling to breed&born it."[19] It certainly works in the lovely "mariposa" where "love is fine and full" and "here the fight rewards the future."[20]

Remarks on Sekou's creative and even inventive use of imagery are numerous, and we have cited examples relative to the sowing of seed, yields, and harvest in chapter 2 on labor. In his landmark publication, *Salted Tongues*, Badejo judges that whether in prose or poetry Sekou deploys a rich and powerful imagery, in the same way Shaka, King of the Amazulu, or Toussaint L'Ouverture "must have deployed their conquering armies, with style and intelligence."[21] So even in prose there is strong imagery: homespun, sometimes rough-hewn, but graphic and effective and consonant with the author's intoxication with what is native. Freddie is "calm as the eye of a hurricane" or at one time "the veins in his forehead (are) bulging like enraged fingers." The images are fresh and functional. He has to be careful, though, not to be carried away in the fiction less he obscures character while luxuriating in the poetic.

Typically, Sekou's imagery is drawn from folkways and the natural and social environment. When in "Nativity" he writes of "the Flamboyant sees its period" the emotional effect is stunning as he sustains the imagery of birth and fertility and bold redness. A different kind of image and also a gem is found in "el malecon" in *The Salt Reaper*: "my caribbean sea is soft / like a kitten's kiss of licks upon itself." In these lines, alliteration, onomatopoeia, and internal rhymes all combine for a pleasing effect.

Sekou reserves his most telling and gripping imagery for political subjects, slavery, mismanagement at home, oppressive overlordship rule, and the independence agenda. Examples are readily drawn from any piece. Describing the black pens of human cargo we are told: "wee crawled to the bucket of shit, fecal of the alone / of the many / of all the heavens & hells from coast to mountain boast."[22] *Born Here* is studded similarly with abrasive and vitriolic imagery which plays out the poet's disgust of the political scene. Colonial rule has his home "Tied to the tentacles / Of paternal parasites." And, consequently, it has become decadent needing to be rebuilt "from menstrual blood and decay." It had to be rescued from "ice-filth designs"[23] that is, foreign northern solutions because under the status quo, there were "Boils all over the people / Pus running over the face of / the land." He blames the situation on the supine complacence of sleepy politicians and their bankrupt policy of "imported chicken and pirated TV re-runs." The picture is one of economic and cultural dependence of an emasculated homeland with "Strange animals ... eating away / The genitals of our tomorrow." In Rasta tones, the poem is called "Downpression," a word that features in his nation tongue lexicon.

Sekou is fully conscious of the power of images to influence consciousness and behavior, which is why he crafts his pieces so carefully. So he rejects bleeding gods,

Hanging around on plastic crosses
Terrorizing the poor
With helpless images of redemption
To be found in far off places . . .[24]

Images can both teach and terrorize; Sekou hopes that his own imagery teaches. He bends Christian images to his will saluting youths "born in a bethlehem of ghettos."[25] Finally on imagery, he uses "salt" as a remarkable extended metaphor in *The Salt Reaper* to evoke the brutality of slavery "through briny ages,"[26] but the irony and complexity do not escape him for salt is also a preserver and seasoner. Salt hurts and heals, for the speaking salt pond tell us, "it was I who seasoned the brine of ages in your pool of blood." Sekou uses what I call the plain statement (for want of a more felicitous term) to powerful effect. Such statements brook of no demur, dissent or compromise. It is like God saying, "Let there be light" and he was dead-right. Here are a few examples conveying his view of the justice system as it affects the oppressed and poor, he says "The farce of law / Lies heavy on the land."[27] It may be a statement of disgust at self-loathing: "Just cut the cold shit, man!" where the monosyllabic words shorn of rhetoric ambush the reader into agreement. This "Nativity" line also exemplifies the technique with added emphasis from the internal rhyme: "Black rage cannot be caged."

This shows the poet deliberately crafting lines; and not to be missed is the epithet "cold" preceding "shit"; it evokes and picks up "metropole," which appears a few lines earlier, and speaks of source of influence. *The Salt Reaper* contains two such lines on his pet theme of freedom, one already referred to earlier in the book: "Freedom not paid for is forfeit"[28] and "Freedom is my bitch in heat."[29] The former admitting the struggle for freedom requires sacrifice and the latter gilded by a sexual metaphor, illustrating his pull toward and pursuit of freedom.

Sekou employs mainly free verse with scant rhyme, and one hardly expects the dominance of the iambic pentameter and classical forms from a poet whose model is his fathers "Dancing in the shadow of iguanas." Significantly, his poem on aesthetics is the penultimate one in *Born Here* as though it were a footnote, and it is followed, again significantly by "Old Words":

Be advised
Not to stand in our way,
We are stepping razors
And will stand in your throat /
We are cutting lasers
. . .
We will stand up
Rugged and refined

Words like "rugged," "razors," "lasers" and "cutting" are instructive, and there are hints of intolerance with standard niceties of language except when it suits him. He is not only rugged but refined, and he can be elegiac as befits the mood. Against this background one better appreciates his rhyming policy. You will look in vain for poems that rhyme in the conventional sense in *37 Poems*, his 2005 volume. It is fair to say that occasionally the poetry resembles prose chopped up, but on closer study, the lines suit his voice and modulation, allowing him to capture tones and moods. This is what is sometimes referred to as voice print. Where Sekou rhymes, he uses it for special purpose—to underline his particular position and philosophy. My favorite example is in "For 17 Cricketers" in *Born Here*:

> Look how they went there
> To play a game
> To shame all Africans.

The combination of end and internal rhymes is engaging, and the rhymes convey contrasting attitude in the trivialness of "play a game" against the weight of "shame." And in "Overstanding" there is touching pathos in "And / Jacqueline Creft / who left so soon" where "left" is a euphemism for death. (I would contend, and have done so, that Jacqueline's elevation to the Caribbean firmament alongside Butler, Garvey, and Castro may have been a bit premature.)[30] The occasional end rhyme also appears as in this couplet ending "nation suite 1" in *37 Poems*:

> when you don't know the land of father's unstated claim
>
> not even the notion of mother's one and only name

which Sekou uses (conventionally) to climax the poem and clinch the thought. But these are rare exceptions.

Sekou puns and builds double meanings delightfully, and he distorts words and coins phrases to serve his satirical purpose to the point of cynicism and damning dismissal. "Nativity" has a number of examples: "In the Kitchener cooking black-eye peas" is a reference to calypsonian Lord Kitchener as well as the obvious cooking/kitchen matter; "hueman beings" refers to the colored folks (humans) who combine to attack "anti-man" systems; in "crime ministers" (we are intended to read prime ministers with a deadly twist); catching "aids" is merely a pluralizing of aid to be derived from the US Caribbean Basin Initiative. Some of the bold imaginative creations surprise, which is part of the delight as in the satirical, "when Paul on the road to de-mask us"; and for a similar satirical play-on-word/double meaning from "Nativity":

> we People

> still wanting to
> federate somehow
> & still not fed up
> with the betraying waste/

Reference to a "roman massa" in *The Salt Reaper* is intriguing but perhaps unsettling for sensitive Roman Catholics. He is obviously referring to the Pope and mass, but "massa" set him forth as an authoritarian ruler with resonances of slavery. The final example is from *37 Poems* where "nether/lands"[31] is at once one and two words that effectively suggest a fractured island and the ambiguity of ownership. Mature crafting of this nature refutes any idea of Sekou as a free "versifier" spinning casual lines. In her introduction to "Nativity," Gumbs correctly recognized that "nearly every word and/or verse is loaded with multiple meanings."

Close to his punning, one can place Sekou's skill at mocking irony. An outstanding example is a reference to the Middle Passage in "Nativity":

> from the back of a gauntlet of sharks
> bloodstaintrailing the Good
> > Ship
> > Jesus

All this blood and slavery and Jesus are richly ironic and even cynical. Another of my favorites from *Born Here* (repeated in this volume) is:

> I believe in God
> But that is not right

in connection with the cost of protecting the Pope is in the same category. There is also a heavy touch of satire and irony to

> chicken leg & rum drunk
> when election-time come like slave X-mas.[32]

Peasants, not just popes, feel the Sekou sting.

In his aesthetics, Sekou blazes trails, and one is consequently obliged to be inventive in analyzing his techniques. This is why I am designating this final technique as the *packaging of words* and sounds sweeping up to a climax or crescendo. I touched on this *en passant* in discussing alliteration, but it is worthy of discrete consideration. We begin with "Nativity," where in the manner of Langston Hughes he speaks of rivers, capturing a rolling rhythm as of the sound of waters deep and fulsome

> Kingly
>   like rivers
>   Niles&Nigers of rivers
>   &Amazons&Mississippis of rivers
> flowing thunder deep *rios* of rivers
>   like my soul's been running
>   deep

where the visual matches sense and sound as it meanders on the page. Sometimes he portrays climaxes, which he reaches skillfully using repetition (another technique) and achieves them with near orgasmic delight:

> meh head hutting meh
> meh foot
> meh bellaaaaaaaaaaaaaaaaaaaaaaaaaaaaaaay

Here he enjoys culture like "manponasweetwoman country / We comiiiiiiiin' Togetherrrrrrrr." He could also use it to express anger as when he climaxes one outburst with "allyouracistmothafuckerrrrrrrs!" where the abrasive is conduit for his anger against apartheid. We end with a more sedate and sensual example from *37 Poems* about the naked muse of poetry:

> she wears . . .   from the shower
>   from the rain
>   from the zinc-curtained bath
>   from the basin's marble terrain
> wears herself, unrobed, *sin verguenza*
> the perfume of water[33]

Wordsworth has rightly said that we murder to dissect, but it was necessary to isolate some of Sekou's crafting techniques to get some understanding of his creative power. It must be said that he employs a combination of these techniques as suits and befits the moment. They help us understand how he achieves such persuasive power and with emotional effect and how his personal anger is controlled (barely sometimes) and why he is not overly preachy although he pulpits forth his poems.

We have already identified religions of African origin, and the beauty of
tight and loose
curled
hair
full
lips
kisssweet

should not be overlooked. But it is also a continent of original achievements in architecture, education, medicine, industry and the arts. There is much to be proud of in Africa, so its sons and daughters do not have to kneel

> for them to tv you How Europe
> > Underde-
> > ve l op
> > Africa
> in the rageful Destruction of Black
> > > > CIVILIZATION[34]

It is generally true that we cannot totally separate the mode from the message. It is especially true of Sekou. He is the "knower-poet," as Badejo calls him,[35] and much of his work is connected with history including contemporary developments. Sekou's knowledge, for instance, of the paraphernalia of US imperialism such as the Monroe Doctrine, the big stick policy, manifest destiny, dollar diplomacy, and the Caribbean Basin Initiative, among others, is critical for carrying out his liberation agenda. His artistic tools are fashioned and honed to deal with that kind of repressive ideology and action. It is reaction and resistance to this stifling and hypocritical perspective that produced imagery such as "ice-filth designs," "cold sores," "fangs," "bat," and "rape," which dramatize the rapaciousness of neoimperialism descending from the north and from Europe.

Equally, his familiarity with the heroes of Caribbean liberation history, whether Butler or Bishop, allow him to reject the psychology of dependency, so mind metaphors such as "imported and pirated TV reruns." These symbolize native potential and promise of "seminal seeds / for bountiful tomorrows." When I write in chapter six of the internal consistency in Sekou's work, therefore, this includes both content and artistic strategies. Sekou himself recognizes the marriage of the art and the labor. How else can one interpret these lines from *Maroon Lives* in particular:

Look what they did
To the lyrics
Of the song
To the rhythm of our labor[36]

with their pathos and mini-jeremiad as he contemplates the sabotaging of the Grenadian revolution by Caribbean sprats and external killer sharks. We end where we began, for Sekou has amply illustrated that:

I have watched my fathers
Dancing in the shadow of iguanas

The history of Africa is also woven into the fabric of his work, into its rhythm and its very grammar.

RECOGNIZING SEKOU

Fabian Badejo's *Salted Tongues – Modern Literature in St. Martin* is by definition not about Sekou, but it is a shining tribute to his work. He is certainly the colossus of the island's literature as a versatile creative writer, essayist, and publisher. In my introduction to that book, I made this comment which bears repeating here. "It would be erroneous to say that Sekou is the literature of St. Martin but the hyperbole is pardonable." When Dr. Wim Rutgers says that Badejo has contributed significantly to filling a gap in Caribbean literature,[1] he is saying by implication that Sekou has carved out an important niche in Caribbean literature. Sekou is at least central to the modern literature of St. Martin, and its body of literature is big for a small place.

The central themes of this author's work are liberation, revolution, and independence. For him the miseries (not only the victories to claim) of St. Martin, the Caribbean, the Americas, and the African *provincia* are miseries that will not let him rest. Carter's famous statement: "I do not sleep to dream, but dream to change the world" is eminently applicable to Sekou. It has been suggested that Sekou has been writing 50 years behind his time and that he is going over ground trodden by Carter and Brathwaite, the model resistance poets.[2] That he is writing in the supposed post-independence or "post-colonial" age does not make him irrelevant. A number of colonies by whatever designations still exist in the Caribbean, and so does oppression even when it has assumed new visages even in independent countries. Indeed, the policies of institutions such as the World Bank and the IMF, which are managed by metropolitan countries, have negatived independence in some of our countries and further pauperized the poor.

Sekou's is not just the voice of the mini- and the micro-Caribbean but the voice of the oppressed everywhere:

> in the Caribbean, in 'Tortured fragments,' in 'Los otros americanos,' in 'abu ghraib,' or 'from a home in kigali/ morning prayers in kosovo/a pall pot brew in kampuchea'—all of us involved in the struggle to find ourselves in this world.[3]

And who is to say that apartheid does not exist in a new guise elsewhere because it ended in South Africa? And who is to say that racism in Britain and elsewhere ended in Brixton? The news belies this. Incredible as it is, black students have recently been ordered to sit in the back of the bus in Louisiana. Sekou's "dark man" appears suddenly, like a serial insurgency brewing time-traveler in *The Salt Reaper*

and *37 Poems*, rallying the downtrodden:
>   in cities & countries
>   in territories & everywhere
>   across oceans & piss puddles & all
>   dredging ahead in time. soul&sciences.
>   holdfast, my loved ones
>   from mississippi to *cité soleil*
>   from afro-colombiano to darfur
>   from middle region to port morrisby[4]

Journalist as he is, many of his poems continue to reflect contemporary realities—whether about Chinese coal miners or Filipina domestic workers—which give them an immediacy and an undoubted relevance. This makes his voice a fresh one, and this is helped by references to the digital age as Allen-Agostini has helpfully pointed. Imagery still comes from nature and the culture, but words like "matrix," "digicam," "download," "e-asked," and "imbed" from US wars of adventure find their way into new writings. Writing of food from Beijing lines like "great wall of bones rising out of red flesh spiced and no rice for me" archly appear. As long as domination of man by man exists, as long as Sekou remains an avid scholar of the world, as long as an imperative exists to shape the consciousness of a people whose true destiny is liberation, his body of work is relevant. And poems on Iraq come as no surprise whether you agree with his editorializing or not. For him "occupation" is occupation, in St. Martin or Iraq.

Beyond any propagandization purpose, Sekou evinces a genuine interest in children and their education. From the emergent hip-hop streets of urban USA in *Moods for Isis* and *Images in The Yard*, to the present state of his father's village in "middle region" from *37 Poems*, references to children and youth and their need for instruction are numerous in his work. As long as he and his work survive, no one needs ask in a spirit of despair: "Who will sing a song for the children?" This is all consonant with his holistic view of life and society and indeed of his good sense and commitment to St. Martin society in the first place.

Poetry does not sell well in the Caribbean region partly because the rank and file regard it as esoteric and unrelated to their lives. Pursuant to his purpose as missionary rather than as marketer, Sekou has made his poems accessible through his riveting performances. Most of his reviewers have remarked on the power of his art as a performer. He stands with Linton Kwesi Johnson and dub poets of Jamaica such as the deceased Mickey Smith and perhaps above them in performance poetry. He entertains his audience and engages them with their history and cultural reality. Teaching, which some see metaphorically as theater, can take a leaf out of Sekou's book and better yet the "nation" should buy the book.

The translation of Sekou's poems into a number of languages means that his art, ideas, and revolutionary thrust are available to readers outside the Anglophone Caribbean. The languages are Spanish, Dutch, German, and Chinese—an interesting mix. With Chinese in particular, Sekou has gone places and may have done so ahead of most Caribbean poets and has thereby emphasized his international stature.

Acceptability is linked with accessibility, and it does appear that as a prophet (I do not use the word figuratively), Sekou has earned the confidence of his people. The Commissioner of Education and Culture and other St. Martin dignitaries have been known to attend his readings, some of which draw crowds of over 100 people. On the wider stage, some of his works have become text books not only in St. Martin but in the USA. Institutions of higher learning, including Cleveland State University, Kenyon College, Canada's York University, and the University of St. Martin have prescribed Sekou's work as reading in English, literature and Caribbean studies courses. He received further international recognition when he was among four persons from the Windward Islands which UNESCO honored for their work in promoting and validating the creole or indigenous language. As a leading poet in the mini-Caribbean, Sekou has had wide exposure across the world in the performance of his work. It has taken him to far China as a visiting fellow to the Hong Kong Baptist University, and he has read, literally on the streets of Medellin and in the classroom at the University of the West Indies (UWI). Writing in the *Sunday Gleaner* of November 30, 1986, one academic thought that his work deserved a wide Caribbean audience. Yet another UWI academic Professor Carolyn Cooper, who was guest speaker at *The Salt Reaper* book launch, was highly complimentary.

Further recognition comes when persons of artistic stature choose to read Sekou's work. This happened in Harlem in 2006, when St. Kitts-connected New York actor Keith David staged a reading of Caribbean poetry. The Emmy award-wining actor and writer included Sekou among a galaxy of writers of the likes of Césaire, Garvey, Claude McKay, and Walcott. Not bad company for the St. Martin artist. In May 2007, Sekou was declared a "Distinguished Visitor" by the Dominican municipality of La Romana, where he presented a paper on the socio-economic and cultural contributions of immigrants from St. Martin and other eastern Caribbean islands to the city, which was celebrating its centenary. (The Dominican Republic consulate in St. Martin had already presented Sekou with a "Recognition for literary excellence in the service of Caribbean unity" in 2003.) Again in 2007, The Caribbean Tourism Organization presented Sekou with its Award of Excellence in New York for his "Dedication to the Global Promotion of Caribbean Culture and Literature through Storytelling, Poetry and Publishing."

The decision of St. Martin institutions of learning to invite Sekou to read and to discuss his poetry with students is a significant act of recognition. The students are not press-ganged into this activity as their alertness, alacrity, and willingness to participate suggest. Participation has included selecting poems and fictions for exam reading. This kind of activity guarantees sustainable recognition, and given Sekou's passion for the societal education of the children, this response is only reasonable.

Another dimension of recognition derives from the publication of Sekou's work outside the "comfort alcoves" of the House of Nehesi Publishers (HNP). At the beginning of 2006, the St. Martin media reported with some euphoria that Sekou's "Liberation Theology" was published in *The Oxford Book of Caribbean Verse* (2005) edited by Dr. Stewart Brown of Birmingham University and Dr. Mark McWatt of the University of the West Indies. The *Encyclopaedia of Caribbean Literature* (2006), published in the United Kingdom and the United States by Greenwood Press, has Sekou within its covers. A few months later, Beck reviews *The Salt Reaper* in the March issue of *World Literature Today*, comparing Sekou's work not only to the "revolutionary political rhetoric" of Linton Kwesi Johnson but also to "the lush, esoteric wordplay of Dylan Thomas" and the love poem "home again" is declared to be in "the manner of e.e. cummings." Then his poem "shiphole II winternights" appeared in the Summer 2006 edition of *Boundary 2*, a reportedly critical journal of literature and culture published by Duke University Press. These were only a few of an unprecedented rush of critical reviews and publications of Sekou's work in national, regional and international media, in less than one year. Sekou himself justifiably believes that "A national literature is also being developed by the way we are perceived abroad through all of our ongoing cultural arts production."[5] As one whose work is also published in the Oxford book, I appreciate the sentiment about external authoritative endorsement. It is important, but it is also worth observing that Sekou's work has an internal consistency and artistic integrity that give it inherent value; he creates credible emotional effects. He has arrived on his own steam, and it is good that distinguished others recognize this.

Having mentioned the "comfort alcoves" of HNP, I need to advise that Sekou's work is exposed to the critical scrutiny of a range of scholars and artists who certainly go beyond backslapping. Peters-McKenzie in reviewing *Love Songs Make You Cry* finds him a fantastic story teller possessing a powerful imagination with matching linguistic tools. She, however, detects shades of subjectivity as the author becomes so absorbed in the dramatic that he "appears to lose touch with objectivity."[6] Van Enckevort has a positive appreciative eye for *The Salt Reaper*, but she chides Sekou ever so gently but firmly for limiting empowerment to the dark man alone. In a searching critique of *Brotherhood of the Spurs*, Andy Gross detects stilted and overly formalized language, clichéd incidents, and verbiage crammed into scenarios. He charges

> There are also moments when Sekou would do well to lessen the control over his characters, and allow them freedom to surprise us by throwing curves or acting against the grain. Again Sekou's powers as an observer, his journalistic streak, sometimes leaves his writing not so much devoid of much passion as emotion.[7]

On the need for independence of characters, I concur, less so on the emotion matter because such instances seem few. But as Gross himself concludes, "these are minor points, like telling a mermaid she is wet behind the ears even while she is dazzling you." Sekou obviously appreciates this frankness, and it is good for his art.

As an author, with a message aimed at social and political change, Sekou will not make comfortable reading for everyone, as Liverpool has intimated in the introduction to *The Salt Reaper*. What is important is that he remains polemical without being unduly preachy. In this we have the nod of Unigwe of University of Leiden for whom Sekou manages on the whole to pass on his messages without sacrificing his art.[8] This is important, for even if the quest for independence remains unfulfilled in the process, Sekou has given to St. Martin, the Caribbean, and the world a respectable body of literature. I would like to see his epic poem, "Nativity" on the UWI reading list for the course "Caribbean Studies." It would be enriched thereby. As I wrote in a *Caribbean Contact* review of *Nativity* in 1988,

> Sekou's culture is encyclopaedic in scope encompassing the songs of the children—the rastaman, Kwesi Johnson's dread beat and blood from Jama-London, Cuban Guillén, Aztec divinities, the folk satire of Louise Bennett and Walcott's tough meld of emotion, and ratiocination—all finely textured.[9]

Back to the reviewers. It is they who have helped to establish Sekou as an abiding force in literature. And in their collective minds, there is no doubt about the value of his contribution. Let me give the penultimate word to one of them:

> This talented author has irrefutably proven himself as a rapidly rising star in the bright firmament of Caribbean writers.[10]

Even if Lasana M. Sekou is no longer perceived as a miracle, he is, at least, a wonder; and his name already written in flamboyant red is underscored by the establishment of the House of Nehesi Publishers which provides opportunities for other writers. Creative writing flourishes within his orbit.

Notes

Preface

[1] Dennis Scott, "Harboursong," *Strategies* (Jamaica: Sandberry Press, 1989) 9.

[2] Winnie Oyoko Loving, "St. Croix Lifestyles," *The St. Croix Avis* 25 Feb. 1987: 5+.

[3] Dr. Joanna W. A. Rummens, "Introduction," *Brotherhood of the Spurs*, Lasana M. Sekou (Philipsburg: House of Nehesi Publishers, 1997) *xiv*.

Chapter 1

[1] Linda Taylor, "Introduction," *Moods for Isis – Picture poems of Love & Struggle*, Lasana M. Sekou (H.H. Lake) (New York: Self-published, 1978) 4.

[2] Lasana M. Sekou (H.H. Lake), *Moods for Isis – Picture poems of Love & Struggle* (New York: Self-published, 1978) 86.

[3] Sekou, *Moods* 74.

[4] Rummens *xiii*.

[5] Taylor 5.

[6] Lasana M. Sekou, *Nativity and Monologues for Today* (Philipsburg: House of Nehesi, 1988) 20+.

[7] Tabish Khair, "Introduction," *37 Poems*, Lasana M. Sekou (Philipsburg: House of Nehesi Publishers, 2005) *xi*.

[8] Lasana M. Sekou, *Images in the Yard* (New York: House of Nehesi, 1983) 13, 15.

[9] Sekou, *Images* 5.

[10] Sekou, *Images* 71.

[11] Lasana M. Sekou, *For the Mighty Gods . . . An Offering* (New York: House of Nehesi, 1982) 39.

[12] Lasana M. Sekou, *The Salt Reaper – Poems from the flats* (Philipsburg: House of Nehesi Publishers, 2004) 75.

[13] Sekou, *Moods* 70.

[14] Lasana M. Sekou, *Mothernation – Poems from 1984 to 1987* (Philipsburg: House of Nehesi, 1991) 69.

[15] Sekou, *Mothernation* 70.

[16] Daniella Jeffry, "Introduction," *Love Songs Make You Cry*, Lasana

156

M. Sekou (Philipsburg: House of Nehesi, 1989) *xii*.

[17] Rummens *xi*.

[18] Sekou, *Born Here* 29.

[19] Fabian A. Badejo, "Introduction," *Born Here*, Lasana M. Sekou (Philipsburg: House of Nehesi, 1986) *xi*.

[20] Sekou, *Mighty Gods* 48.

[21] Sekou, *Salt Reaper* 98.

[22] Sekou, *37 Poems* 8.

Chapter 2

[1] Lasana M. Sekou, *Brotherhood of the Spurs* (Philipsburg: House of Nehesi Publishers, 1997) 71.

[2] Sekou, *Moods* 60.

[3] Lasana M. Sekou, *Big Up St. Martin – Essay and Poem* (Philipsburg: House of Nehesi Publishers, 1999) 13.

[4] Sekou, *Nativity* 17.

[5] Sekou, *37 Poems* 13.

[6] Sekou, *Salt Reaper* 47.

[7] Sekou, *Salt Reaper* 48.

[8] Sekou, *Spurs* 31.

[9] Sekou, *Spurs* 29.

[10] Sekou, *Spurs* 31.

[11] Sekou, *Mothernation* 3.

[12] Sekou, *Born Here* 113.

[13] Sekou, *Moods* 55.

[14] Lasana M. Sekou, *Maroon Lives – For Grenadian freedom fighters* (New York: House of Nehesi, 1983) 26.

[15] Sekou, *Nativity* 2.

[16] Sekou, *Salt Reaper* 84.

[17] Sekou, *Salt Reaper* 36.

[18] Sekou, *Salt Reaper* 50.

[19] Hollis "Chalkdust" Liverpool, PhD, "Introduction," *The Salt Reaper – Poems from the flats*, Lasana M. Sekou (Philipsburg: House of Nehesi Publishers, 2004) *xiii*.

[20] Sekou, *Salt Reaper* 36.

[21] Lasana M. Sekou, *Quimbé – Poetics of Sound* (Philipsburg: House of Nehesi, 1991) 101.

[22] Sekou, *Images* 31.

[23] Sekou, *Moods* 29.

[24] Sekou, *Quimbé* 94.

[25] Sekou, *37 Poems* 5.

[26] Sekou, *Mothernation* 87.

[27] Sekou, *Mighty Gods* 15.

[28] Sekou, *Moods* 26.

[29] Sekou, *Images* 23.

[30] Sekou, *Images* 49.

[31] Sekou, *Mothernation* 17.

[32] Sekou, *Mothernation* 92.

[33] Sekou, *Maroon Lives* 78.

[34] Sekou, *37 Poems* 5.

[35] Sekou, *Born Here* 44.

[36] Sekou, *Moods* 90.

[37] Sekou, *Moods* 88.

[38] Sekou, *Born Here* 77.

[39] Sekou, *Born Here* 62.

[40] Sekou, *Big Up St. Martin* 24.

[41] Sekou, *Big Up St. Martin* 13.

[42] Sekou, *Images* 84.

[43] Sekou, *Born Here* 114.

[44] L.A. Perez, Jr., (quoted in) "St. Maarten/St. Martin Mass Media's Role in the Move Towards Independence – Recommendations Being Followed by *Newsday*," Lasana M. Sekou, *The Independence Papers – Readings on a New Political Status for St. Maarten/St. Martin, Volume I*, Lasana M. Sekou, Oswald Francis, Napolina Gumbs, eds. (Philipsburg: House of Nehesi, 1990) 102.

[45] Sekou, *Born Here* 136.

[46] Sekou, *Independence Papers* 16.

[47] Sekou, *Nativity* 19.

[48] Sekou, *Salt Reaper* 4.

Chapter 3

[1] Sekou, *Moods* 44.

[2] Sekou, *Maroon Lives* 29.

[3] Sekou, *Born Here* 107.

[4] Sekou, *Images* 28.

[5] Sekou, *Images* 31.

[6] Sekou, *Maroon Lives* 17.

[7] Sekou, *Salt Reaper* 95.

[8] Sekou, *Salt Reaper* 91.

[9] Sekou, *Nativity* 10, 14.

[10] Sekou, *Images* 128.

[11] Sekou, *Maroon Lives* 3.

[12] Sekou, *Mothernation* 31.

[13] Sekou, *Born Here* 125.

[14] Sekou, *Mighty Gods* 26.

[15] *Maroon Lives* 12.

[16] Sekou, *Maroon Lives* 13.

[17] Sekou, *Maroon Lives* 24.

[18] Sekou, *Born Here* 132.

[19] Sekou, *Maroon Lives* 4+.

[20] Sekou, *Born Here* 131.

[21] Fabian A. Badejo, "Revolution as Poetic Inspiration: Grenada in *Maroon Lives* by Lasana Sekou" (Caribbean Studies Association Conference, St. Kitts, 1984) 2.

[22] Sekou, *Maroon Lives* 4.

[23] Sekou, *Maroon Lives* 31.

[24] Sekou, *Maroon Lives* 29.

[25] Sekou, *Maroon Lives* 21.

[26] Sekou, *Maroon Lives* 7.

[27] Sekou, *Images* 8.

[28] Sekou, *Salt Reaper* 8.

[29] Lisa Allen-Agostini, "S'maatin Poems," *The Caribbean Review of Books* Feb. (2006): 27.

[30] Sekou, *Maroon Lives* 19.

[31] Sekou, *Images* 19.

[32] Sekou, *Maroon Lives* 14.

[33] Lisa Allen-Agostini 27.

[34] Sekou, *Big Up St. Martin* 9+.

[35] Julio Meit, "In 1966-67, Jose Lake, Sr. Was Writing About It," *Independence Papers* 20+.

[36] Fabian Adekunle Badejo, *Salted Tongues – Modern Literature in St.Martin* (Philipsburg: House of Nehesi Publishers, 2003) 20.

[37] Lasana M. Sekou, ed., *National Symbols of St. Martin – A Primer* (Philipsburg: House of Nehesi Publishers, 1996) 29+.

[38] Sekou, *37 Poems* 36.

[39] Sekou, *Mighty Gods* 77.

[40] Sekou, *Moods for Isis* 34.

[41] Sekou, *Images* 23.

[42] Sekou, *Moods for Isis* 74.

[43] Sekou, *37 Poems* 7.

[44] Sekou, *Quimbé* 83.

[45] Sekou, *Born Here* 45.

[46] Sekou, *Images* 108.

[47] Sekou, *Images* 75.

[48] Sekou, *Images* 73.

[49] Sekou, *Big Up St. Martin* 1.

[50] *Maroon Lives* 30.

[51] Sekou, *Moods for Isis* 26.

[52] Sekou, *Images* 105.

[53] Sekou, *Salt Reaper* 15.

[54] Sekou, *Mighty Gods* 4.

[55] Sekou, *Mighty Gods* 8.

[56] Sekou, *Born Here* 44.

Chapter 4

[1] Ismail Serageldin, ed., *Culture and Development at the Millennium: The Challenge and Response* (New York: McGraw Hill, 1998) 9.

[2] Ira Mathur, "The Phoenix Speaks Again," *Trinidad Guardian*, 23 Sept. 1999: 9.

[3] Rex Nettleford, "Caribbean Cultural Identity: The Case of Jamaica, An Essay in Cultural Dynamics (Jamaica: Institute of Jamaica, 1978).

[4] Ervin Beck, "The Salt Reaper: Poems from the Flats," *World Literature Today*, 58 (2006) 58.

[5] Jeffry, *Love Songs* ix.

[6] "Time for Action: The Report of the West Indian Commission" (Barbados: The West Indian Commission, 1992) 265.

[7] Sekou, *Nativity* 4.

[8] Sekou, *Big Up St. Martin* 10.

[9] Sekou, *Born Here* 146.

[10] Sekou, *Salt Reaper* 35.

[11] Sekou, *Spurs* 51.

[12] Sekou, *Nativity* 19+.

[13] Sekou, *Spurs* 116.

[14] Sekou, *Nativity* 39.

[15] Sekou, *Nativity* 20.

[16] Sekou, *Moods for Isis* 44.

[17] Sekou, *Born Here* 44.

[18] Sekou, *Born Here* 40.

[19] Sekou, *Born Here* 40.

[20] Sekou, *Spurs* 14.

[21] Liverpool, *Salt Reaper xiv*.

[22] Sekou, *Moods for Isis* 59.

[23] Sekou, *Nativity* 10+.

[24] Napolina Gumbs, "Introduction," *Nativity and Monologues for Today* (Philipsburg: House of Nehesi, 1988) *xi*.

[25] Maria van Enckevort, "'I' the Female, 'I' the White Outsider Looking at *The Salt Reaper* by Lasana M. Sekou," *The Daily Herald* http://www.the daily herald.com/news/daily/h153/book 153.ht.m/

[26] Sekou, *Nativity* 7.

[27] Sekou, *Mothernation* 99.

[28] Derek Walcott, *Collected Poems 1948-84* (London: Faber and Faber, 1992) 33.

[29] Sekou, *Nativity* 9.

[30] Farrukh Dhondy, *C.L.R. James: Cricket, The Caribbean and World Revolution* (London: Weidenfeld & Nicolson) 2001.

[31] Sekou, *Moods for Isis* 32.

[32] Fabian Badejo, "L. Sekou, St. Maarten's first Revolutionary Poet," *Newsday* 24 May 1983: 9+.

[33] Wycliffe Smith, "Born here," *Amigoe, Ñapa* 13 Sept. 1986.

[34] Sekou, *Nativity* 28.

Chapter 5

[1] Badejo, *Salted Tongues* 18+.

[2] Howard A. Fergus, "New Caribbean Identity Born," *Caribbean*

Contact Oct. 1988: 15.

[3] Howard A. Fergus, "Introduction," *Salted Tongues: Modern Literature in St.Martin*, Fabian Adekunle Badejo (Philipsburg: House of Nehesi Publishers, 2003) *xiii*.

[4] J.C. Aboud, "Conquistador" *The New Voices*, XVI: 32 (1988): 105.

[5] Dr. Howard Fergus, "Sekou's work called the cultural "miracle" of St. Martin," *St. Maarten/St. Martin Newsday* 15-21 Nov. 1991: 5+.

[6] Sekou, *Mothernation* 4.

[7] Sekou, *37 Poems* 9.

[8] Sekou, *Nativity* 17.

[9] Fergus, "New Caribbean Identity Born" 15.

[10] Smith, *Ñapa* 13 Sept. 1986.

[11] Van Enckevort, "'I' the Female, 'I' the White Outsider ..."

[12] Tabish Khair, "Introduction: Reasons to Live," *37 Poems* (Philipsburg: House of Nehesi Publishers) *x*.

[13] Sekou, *Mothernation* 23.

[14] Sekou, *Quimbé* 40.

[15] Joyce Peters-McKenzie, "*Love Songs Make You Cry* stirs emotions that lie too deep for tears," *St. Maarten/St. Martin Newsday* 15-16 Sept. 1899: 2.

[16] Sekou, *Moods for Isis* 21.

[17] Sekou, *Quimbé* 126.

[18] Sekou, *Nativity* 6.

[19] Sekou, *Salt Reaper* 66.

[20] Sekou, *37 Poems* 3.

[21] Badejo, *Salted Tongues* 19.

[22] Sekou, *Salt Reaper* 48.

[23] Sekou, *Born Here* 25.

[24] Sekou, *Images* 31.

[25] Sekou, *Quimbé* 124.

[26] Sekou, *The Salt Reaper* 35.

[27] Sekou, *Images* 84.

[28] Sekou, *Salt Reaper* 7.

[29] Sekou, *Salt Reaper* 25.

[30] Howard A. Fergus, "A Poet of the Human Hurt," *The New Voices* XV: 29-30 (1987): 204.

[31] Sekou, *37 Poems* 12.

[32] Sekou, *Nativity* 18.

[33] Sekou, *37 Poems* 31+.

[34] Sekou, *Nativity* 29.

[35] Badejo, "Revolution as Poetic Inspiration . . ." 5.

[36] Sekou, *Born Here* 44.

[37] Sekou, *Maroon Lives* 31.

Chapter 6

[1] *Salted Tongues* (Book cover blurb).

[2] Allen-Agostini 17.

[3] Liverpool *xv*.

[4] Sekou, *Salt Reaper* 109.

[5] "St. Martin's *Salt Reaper* poem opens *Boundary 2* journal," http:// www.houseofnehesipublish.com/hnpnewsupdate.html.

[6] Peters-McKenzie 3.

[7] Andy Gross "In Our Stories begin Our reality – *Lasana Sekou Dazzles in his Latest Collection of Short Stories: 'The Brotherhood of the Spurs',*" *The St. Maarten Guardian* 1 Dec. 1997: 10+.

[8] Chika Unigwe, "*The Salt Reaper: Poems from the Flats,*" *Postcolonial Text* 2: 3 (2006) http://postcolonial.org/index.php/pct/article/view/ 470/316.

[9] Fergus, "New Caribbean Identity Born" 15.

[10] Rummens *xvi*.

Selected Bibliography
Books by Sekou

Sekou, Lasana M. *37 Poems*. Philipsburg: House of Nehesi Publishers, 2005 (with introduction by Tabish Khair). Poetry.

_____. *The Salt Reaper – Poems from the flats*. Philipsburg: House of Nehesi Publishers, 2004, 2005 (with introduction by Hollis "Chalkdust" Liverpool). Poetry.

_____. *Brotherhood of the Spurs*. Philipsburg: House of Nehesi Publishers, 1997, 2007. Fiction (Short stories).

_____. *Quimbé – Poetics of Sound*. Philipsburg: House of Nehesi, 1991. Poetry.

_____. *Mothernation – Poems from 1984 to 1987*. Philipsburg: House of Nehesi, 1991. Poetry.

_____. *Love Songs Make You Cry*. Philipsburg: House of Nehesi, 1989. Fiction. Sekou's and St. Martin's first published collection of short stories.

_____. *Nativity and Monologues for Today*. Philipsburg: House of Nehesi, 1988. Long poem; drama.

_____. *Born Here*. Philipsburg: House of Nehesi, 1986. Poetry.

_____. *Maroon Lives . . . For Grenadian Freedom Fighters*. New York: House of Nehesi, 1983. Poetry.

_____. *Images in the Yard*. New York: House of Nehesi, 1983. Poetry.

_____. *For the Mighty Gods . . . An Offering*. New York: House of Nehesi, 1982 (with introduction by Amiri Baraka). Poetry.

_____. *Moods for Isis – Picture poems of Love & Struggle*. New York: Self-published. 1978. Poetry.

St. Martin Massive! A Snapshot of Popular Artists. House of Nehesi Publishers, 2000. Edited as a House of Nehesi Publishers Special Edition with an introduction by Sekou.

Sekou, Lasana M., ed. *National Symbols of St. Martin – A Primer*. Philipsburg: House of Nehesi Publishers, 1996, 1997. Primer on history/historical personalities, culture, natural environment; edited with a preface by Sekou.

Sekou, Lasana M., Francis, Oswald, Gumbs, Napolina, eds. *The Independence Papers – Readings on a New Political Status for St. Maarten/St. Martin, Volume 1*. Philipsburg: House of Nehesi, 1990 (with a preface and five articles by Sekou). Articles on politics, education, culture, media.

Booklets

Sekou, Lasana M. *Big Up St. Martin – Essay & Poem*. Philipsburg: House of Nehesi Publishers, 1999. Booklet. Essay on colonialism and independence ("Colony, Territory, or Partner?"); Long poem ("The cubs are in the field").

_____. *Fête – Celebrating Traditional St. Martin Festive Music*. Philipsburg: House of Nehesi Publishers, 1992, 2007 (Revised edition). Companion booklet to *Fête – The first recording of traditional St. Martin festive music* by Tanny & The Boys (LP, cassette 1992; CD 2007).

Sekou in Other Titles

"De Wettige Erfgenamen." *Tropentaal 200 jaar Antilliaanse vertelkunst*. Edited by Wim Rutgers. Amsterdam/Antwerpen: Uitgeverij Contact, 2001: 441+ (Dutch translation of "The Rightful Heirs" from *Love Songs Make You Cry*).

"dm5." *Social Sciences for VSBO/PSVE Schools, Man and Society: Textbook* by Maria Cijntje-van Enckevort et al. Philipsburg: University of St. Martin, 2006: 24.

"Fatty and the Big House." In *Traveller's Literary Companion – The Carribbean*. Edited by James Ferguson. London: In Print Publishing Ltd., 1997: 184+.

"Great Grandmother 'T'." *Swirling Columns of Immigration*. Edited by Aart G. Broek. Curacao: Maduro & Curiel's bank, 1997: 21-23.

Gurus and Griots, Poems and Poets of Africa, of America, and the Caribbean. Edited by Jeanean Gibbs. Palm Tree Enterprises Inc., 1987.

Introduction to *Masquerade*, A Play by Ian Valz. Philipsburg: House of Nehesi, 1988.

"Liberation Theology." *The Oxford Book of Caribbean Verse*. Edited by Stewart Brown and Mark McWatt. London: Oxford University Press, 2005: 319+.

"Our time." *Kadans, literaire ontwikkeling en begrippen*. Edited by Ronnie Severing, Wim Rutgers, Liesbeth Echteld. Curacao: Fundashon pa Planifikashon di Idioma, 2002: 133.

Preface to *In Search of St. Martin's Ancient Peoples – Prehistoric Archaeology* by Dr. Jay B. Haviser (English edition with French translation). Philipsburg: House of Nehesi Publishers, 1995.

Stemmen van Overzee, Toekomstdromen. KIT Publishers, Amsterdam 2004.

"Stirring Gales at the frontier: Charting a new course from St. Martin's Day to National Unification." *The Future Status of Aruba and the Netherlands Antilles*. Edited by Armando Lampe. Aruba: FUNDINI, 1994: 53.

"Visit & Fellowship II," "The blood boil." *Writers of Post-colonial English Speaking Countries*. Hong Kong: IWW, Hong Kong Baptist University, 2004: 111+ (Chinese translation).

Winds Above the Hills. Edited by Wycliffe S. Smith. Philipsburg: St. Maarten Council on the Arts, 1982.

Windward Islands Verse, A Survey of Poetry in the Dutch Windward Islands. Edited by Wycliffe S. Smith. Curacao. N.p., 1981.

"20th Century Herald." *Met eigen stem – herkenningspunten in de letterkunde van de Nederlandse Antillen en Aruba* by Pim Heuvel & Freek van Wel. Assena/Maastricht: Van Gorcum, 1989: 207.

Sekou on the Internet

"Eterno tiempo de siembra. Lasana Sekou (Saint Martin)" http://www.festivaldepoesiademedellin.org/pub.php/en/Multimedia/sekou.htm; "Eterno tiempo de siembra." http://www.youtube.com/watch? v=8l-AON1cqZ4; (Live recital, XIV International Poetry Festival of Medellin. Medellin/Bogota: Colombia, 2004).

"Lasana Sekou Table." *ChickenBones: A Journal*. http://www.nathanielturner.com/lasanasekoutable.htm.

Recital/discussion. Winternachten 2001, 2004. http://www.winternachten.nl/winternachten/index.php?taal=engels.

"This Is." Poetry Africa, 2001. http://www.ukzn.ac.za/cca/pa-2001bios20.html#Lasana%20M%20Sekou(%20St.Martin).

"Tortured Fragments." *International Poetry Festival of Medellin Magazine*. http://www.festivaldepoesiademedellin.org/pub.php/en/Revista/ultimas_ediciones/68_69/sekou.html (a different version of this poem appears in *The Salt Reaper*).

Reviews of Books by Sekou

37 Poems (2005)

Allen-Agostini, Lisa. "S'maatin poems." *The Caribbean Review of Books* Feb. 2006: 17+.

Cooke, Mel. "A poem per square mile." *Jamaica Gleaner* 20 Oct. 2005. http://www.jamaica-gleaner.com/gleaner/20051020/ent/ent1.html.

The Salt Reaper – poems from the flats (2004, 2005)

Allen-Agostini, Lisa. "S'maatin poems." *The Caribbean Review of Books* Feb. 2006: 17+.

Beck, Ervin. "Lasana M. Sekou. The Salt Reaper: Poems from the Flats." *World Literature Today* Mar. 2006: 58. http://www.ou.edu/worldlit/onlinemagazine/2006march/Mar06-19Reviews.pdf.

Cooke, Mel. "Salt of the earth finds voice." *Jamaica Gleaner* 17 Mar. 2006. http://www.jamaica-gleaner.com/gleaner/200603 17/ent/ent4.html.

Allen-Agostini, Lisa. "S'maatin poems." *The Caribbean Review of Books* Feb. 2006. www.meppublishers.com.

Arrendell, Francia. "Lasana Sekou pone en circulación The Salt Reaper." *El Nuevo Hispano* 8 Nov. 2004: 7.

Van Enkevort, Maria, Dr. "'I' the female, 'I' the white outsider, looking at *The Salt Reaper* by Lasana M. Sekou." *The Daily Herald* (2004). http://www.thedailyherald.com/news/daily/h153/book153.html.

De Weever, Pedro. "The Salt Reaper … The invitation is on the table." *The Daily Herald – Weekender* 25 Nov. 2006.

Hanna, Mary. "Sekou writes with 'erotic power'." *Jamaica Gleaner* 5 Nov. 2006. http://www.jamaica-gleaner.com/gleaner/20061105/arts/arts4.html.

Unigwe, Chika. "The Salt Reaper: Poems from the Flats." *Postcolonial Text*, 2.3 (2006). http://postcolonial.org/index.php/pct/article/viewFile/470/316.

Brotherhood of the Spurs (1997, 2007)

Combie, Valerie. "Brotherhood of the Spurs." *The Caribbean Writer* 13 (1999): 273-274. http://rps.uvi.edu/Caribbean-Writer/volume13/brotherhoodofthespurs.html

Gross, Andy. "Special Book Review: In Our Stories Begin Our Reality." *The St. Maarten Guardian* 1 Dec. 1997: 10-11.

Hodge, Charles Borromeo. "*Brotherhood of the Spurs* – A Synopsis." *St. Martin Newsday* 20 Mar. 1998: 5+.

Quimbé – Poetics of Sound (1991)

Jeffry, Daniella. "The 'twin books' symbolize oneness of St. Martin's people." *St. Maarten/St. Martin Newsday.* 29 Nov. 1991: 11.

Peters-McKenzie, Joyce. "*Quimbé*, in which Sekou is a poet of the world." *Newsday* 22-28 May 1992: 6+.

Mothernation – Poems fron 1984 to 1987 (1991)

Jeffry, Daniella. "The 'twin books' symbolize oneness of St. Martin's people." *St. Maarten/St. Martin Newsday.* 29 Nov. 1991: 11.

The Independence Papers – Readings on a New Political Status for St. Maarten/St. Martin, Volume 1, edited with the preface and five essays by Sekou (1990)

De Roo, Jos. "Bundel over onafhankelijkheid – Lasana Sekou: 'St. Martin is ondemocratisch'." *Amigoe/Ñapa* 5 Oct. 1991: 5.

Love Songs Make You Cry (1989)

Casimir, Nel. "Zevende boek Lasana Sekou: Liefde voor S'maatin."*Amigoe* 13 Aug. 1990.

De Roo, Jos. "Patriottisme zonder enig chauvinisme op St. Maarten." *Amigoe/Ñapa* 29 Sept. 1990: 5.

Fergus, Howard, A. "An Exploration of Love." *Caribbean Contact* Sept. 1989: 15.

Fergus, Howard, A. "Lasana M. Sekou. *Love Songs Make You Cry.*" *The Caribbean Writer* 4 (1990): 101+.

Peters-McKenzie, Joyce. "*Love Songs Make You Cry* stirs emotions that lie too deep for tears." *St. Maarten/St. Martin Newsday* 15-16 Sept. 1989.

Ten Holt, Asila. "'Love Songs Make You Cry', by Lasana Mwanza Sekou. Part 1." *La Prensa* 10 Aug. 1990: 10; "Love, Labor, Liberation." (part 2) *La Prensa* 17 Aug. 1990: 10.

Nativity and Monologues for Today (1988)

Fergus, Howard, A. "New Caribbean Identity Born." *Caribbean Contact* Oct. 1988: 15.

Knowles, Roberta Q. "Lasana M. Sekou, Nativity and Dramatic

Monologues for today." *The Caribbean Writer* 3 (1998): 111+.

Born Here (1986)

Fergus, Howard. "Sekou: A Poet of Protest." *Caribbean Contact* Jan. 1987; *The New Voices* XV.29/30 (1987): 200+ (with a different title "A Poet of the Human Hurt").

Jeffry, Daniella. "'Born Here', a turning point in Sekou's development." *St. Maarten/St. Martin Newsday.* 29 Aug. 1986: 1A.

Pereira, Joseph (J.P.). "A maturing voice from St. Maarten." *The Sunday Gleaner* 30 Nov. 1986: 3C.

Smith, WyCliffe. "Born here."*Amigoe/Ñapa* 13 Sept. 1986.

Maroon Lives: Tribute To Grenadian Freedon Fighters (1983)
Images in the Yard (1982)

Westmoore, Peter. "Liberation Fire Drinks Water." *Caribbean Contact* Apr. 1984: 3.

For The Mighty Gods . . . An Offering (1982)
Moods for Isis – Picture poems of Love & Struggle (1978)

Badejo, Fabian. L. Sekou, St. Maarten's first Revolutionary Poet." *Windward Islands Newsday* 24 May 1983: 1A.

Poetry by Sekou in Journals

"Caribbean Journey," "With Vision," *De Gids* 350.7/8 (1990): 586-589.

"Der Makellose Schwarze," "Moskau," "Für Akeem." *Das Gedicht* 9.9 (2001): 65-67.

"Liberation Theology." *The Massachusetts Review* XXXV.3/4 (1994): 540-543.

"Los cimarrones viven," "Traidores," Símbolos." *Del Caribe* II.6 (1986): 43-45.

"shiphole to winternights." *boundary 2 – an international journal of literature and culture* 33: 2 (2006): 6-7.

"Title Deed," "Visit and Fellowship," "Direction II." *Calabash: A Journal of Caribbean Arts and Letters* 1.2 (2001): 78-81. http://www.nyu.edu/calabash/vol1no2/.

"Tortured Fragments," "Fragmentos torturados," "La cultura está acabada." *Prometeo* XXII.68/69 (2004): 135-139.

"Wij Zelf," "We Self." *Catalogus/Catalogue 31 Poetry International Festival* (2000): 148-151.

"1." *Callaloo* 21.3 (1998): 674.

About Sekou (in which his work is discussed)

Badejo, Fabian A. "Introduction to Literature in english in the Dutch Windward Islands." *Callaloo* 21.3 (1998): 676-679.

Badejo, Fabian Adekunle. "Modern Literature In English In The Dutch Windward Islands." *Calabash: A Journal of Caribbean Arts and Letters* 1.2 (2001): 65-77. http://www.nyu.edu/calabash/vol1no2/.

Badejo, Fabian Adekunle. *Salted Tongues – Modern Literature in St.Martin*. Philipsburg: House of Nehesi Publishers, 2003.

Lampe, Armando. "Por la aparición de *Double Play*." *Revista Mexicana del Caribe* 10 (2000): 233-240. http://redalyc.uaemex.mx/redalyc/pdf/128/12801007.pdf.

Rodríguez, Emilio Jorge. "Sekou, Lasana M. (1959-)." In *Encyclopedia of Caribbean Literature, Vol. I – II*. Edited by D.H. Figueredo. Connecticut; London, Greenwood Press, 2006: 739+.

Sample, Jacqueline. "More St. Martin poets reading abroad." *Today* 25 Aug. 2004: 8A.

Windward Islands Verse, A Survey of Poetry in the Dutch Windward Islands. Edited by Wycliffe S. Smith. (St. Martin) 1981.

"Literature of the Dutch Windward Islands." Paper by Wycliffe Smith (Presented to the 46th Congress of Americanists, Amsterdam, Netherlands, July 4-8, 1988).

"*Nativity* – A Tribute To the People of St. Maarten/St. Martin." Address by Daniella Jeffry (Presented at the "Book Party" for *Nativity*, Philipsburg Jubilee Library, June 25, 1988).

"Negritude in the forgotten territories: Lasana Sekou and Aimé Césaire." Paper by Fabian Badejo (Presented to the Senghor Colloquium – "Negritude: Legacy and Present Relevance," Barbados, Oct. 26-27, 2006).

"Rastafari as Image and Voice of Justice in Caribbean Literature." Paper by Kendel Hippolyte (Presented to the 5th Annual St. Martin Book Fair, University of St. Martin, May 31-June 2, 2007).

"Revolution as Poetic Inspiration: Grenada in Maroon Lives by Lasana M. Sekou." Paper by Fabian Badejo (Presented to the IX Annual Conference of the Caribbean Association, St. Kitts, May 29-June 2, 1984).

"Sekou's work called the cultural 'Miracle' of St. Martin." Address by Dr. Howard Fergus (Presented at the "Book Party" for *Quimbé* and *Mothernation*, Philipsburg Jubilee Library, November 2, 1991. In *Newsday* 15-21 Nov. 1991: 5-6).

"The Caribbean Writer and the African Renaissance." Paper by Dr. F. Abiola Irele (Presented to the 5th Annual St. Martin Book Fair, University of St. Martin, May 31-June 2, 2007).

Audio-Visual Productions by Sekou

Fête – The First Recording of Traditional St. Martin Festive Music, by Tanny & The Boys (LP, cassette 1992; CD 2007). Lasana M. Sekou, executive producer; You-May Dormoy, arranger/conductor (Mountain Dove Records/HNP, 1992, 2007).

GEBE Through The Years (dvd, 2005). Lasana M. Sekou, producer; Fabian A. Badejo, director (Woodslave Films/HNP).

How A Power Plant Works (dvd, 2005). Lasana M. Sekou, producer; Fabian A. Badejo, director (Woodslave Films/HNP).